Learning About Dogs

Clicker
Dances
with Dogs

Kay Laurence

LEVEL 3
CLICKER TRAINERS
SPECIALISED RECIPES

Printed in the U.S. and distributed by
Karen Pryor ClickerTraining and Sunshine Books
49 River Street, Waltham, MA 02453
www.clickertraining.com
Sales: U.S. Toll Free 1-800-472-5425
781-398-0754

First edition published in 2002

Learning About Dogs Limited

PO Box 13, Chipping Campden, Glos, GL55 6WX. UK

ISBN 1-890948-29-2

Books in the Clicker Trainers Course series by Kay Laurence:

Clicker Foundation Trainer Level 1

Clicker Novice Trainer Level 2

Book of Challenges for Foundation & Novice trainers

Clicker Intermediate Trainer Level 3

Recipe books for specialised interests:

Clicker Dances with Dogs

Clicker World Obedience Training

and:

Clicker Gundog by Helen Phillips

Clicker Agility for Fun & Fitness by Diana Bird

Click for Grooming, Handling and Treatment by Karen McCarthy

Interactive training games: Gena & GenAbacab

Teaching Dogs Magazine for up to date news on clicker training

www.clickertraining.com

index

INTRODUCTION

Many years ago we used to think teaching a dog to jump was exciting, it certainly rang the changes for dogs that were used to the classic obedience exercises such as heelwork, retrieve, heelwork, stays and even more heelwork.

With the blossoming of clicker training on the heels of the emerging new sport we have really begun to look with much greater depth at what we teach the dogs. We can now teach with precision, defining which leg to move and how to move it, they can learn upwards of 60 movements and poses and the astonishing fact they can remember 60 signals and cues.

This workbook will start you off with ideas of what to teach and some imagination how to teach it. We have made several errors of not giving the dogs learning capacity enough respect - I hope the next generation will find nothing unusual in a dog that can learn 100 moves!

I refer to my own dogs in the exercises, these are my collies and the Gordon Setters, and quite frankly if a Gordon can do it there aren't many dogs that can't. Kiwi was four years old when she started and is still learning new moves at eleven, so not it is not too late.

You do not have to have an ounce of rhythm or sense of dance to teach the dogs "Dances", just regard it as a collective name for fitness training for the dog!

If you are new to clicker training I recommend you read the first two books in the Clicker Trainers series: Foundation and Novice trainer.

They will teach you the key skills, how to capture new behaviours, add cues, build reliability and shaping techniques.

This book covers the specific behaviours intended for heelwork to music, freestyle and dressage type routines.

1 What is Dances?

THE BASIC ELEMENTS OF THE GAME

KEY TO THE SECTIONS AND DIAGRAMS

CLICKER TRAINING IS PERFECT FOR DANCING

WHAT IS DANCES ?

ALL DOGS DANCE

They have natural movement, grace and agility. Watch dogs flirting and the dance is without question. They walk taller, with longer strides. They hold themselves alert, twist and turn, showing off their six packs for their future mate! Girls work as hard as their boys in this game.

They stomp on the spot, walk backwards, stand on their back legs, bounce up and down, slap their front paws on the other dog, in fact, run through a whole repertoire of movements to attract attention. The less attention they get the harder they try! So if you find yourself short of ideas, watch dogs before the bonking begins. Preferably out of season "good friends" as they tend to enjoy the flirt more that the Real Action!

I had a Gordon who would dance on the wind, when he found a particular rich mixture of scents blowing up a gully he would pirouette, twist and turn as if catching blowing leaves.

Our main challenge is to learn how to stimulate these actions (without changing our chemical output) and capture the movements to be able to recall them in time to a piece of music. We also have a lot to learn about flirting canine style!

We are limited by the number of cues we can actually give, not the number of moves the dog can do. I have defined the moves closer to the teaching paradigm not the dancing paradigm so it is easier to teach the dog what a dog does, not what a dancer does.

We have woken up to their potential and have chosen the very pleasurable occupation of capturing their natural dance moves so we can join in together.

Even if you have no set moves or ideas, just getting up and busking to music will activate the dance switch in the dogs, they quickly pick up the mood - busking tends to activate the bark switch as well in mine !

Each section is focused on a particular group of movements, defining exactly what the movements are, how to teach them, suitable cues and variations for individuality.

SOME BASICS TO BEGIN WITH:

THE CUES

This is one activity where un-cued moves can become quite a nuisance, so although the dog may have some great ideas, take note what stimulated the new movement, but don't reward the dog for over use of the creativity muscle at the wrong time. It can lead to havoc in a routine.

We put each behaviour to a simple, single cue, which allows us to combine cues for extra claritiy and creativity. I can ask Kiwi to walk back with a verbal cue, and give the "weave" signal of the bent knee at the same time, cueing a "backwards weave".

The third element of the cue is the location, which can change the context of the cue. If Kiwi is by my side and I give the cue "go round" she will go round me in a small circle, but if she is ten feet away and I say "go round" she will circle in a much larger circle.

Merging the clear actions with location cues gives us brand new moves without using a precious new cue.

Cues can either be:

A. VERBAL

Best used with quiet sounds and small lip movements, but verbal cues can be at a disadvantage if the music is too loud, or the speakers at the level of the dog's ears.

Verbal cues need to be used when the move you want the dog to do is contrary to your body language, for instance you may hold your hand high in the air but want the dog to take a bow.

The dog can be in any place around you where they can hear, it is good for moves when the dog is facing away, not suitable for distance work when that music is blasting.

B. HAND SIGNALS

A lot of the training is done by luring and targeting so hand signals will seem to be the natural cue. But these can be a real distraction for the spectator if they are large and "loud" and catch the eye away from the movement of the dog.

When used carefully, in time to the music and without haste, they can be ideal, but regard all hand signals as part of your choreography not as part of your dog handling. Your arms will be very affected by the music and can change out of all recognition to the dog to different pieces of music.

You will also need to consider where the dog is in relation to the signal. Can they clearly see your hands?

C. BODY LANGUAGE

More than just the hand or arm, but the way you lean, change your balance, tip your head, bend a knee. These are all cues to the dog, the strongest of all and great when used in conjunction with the other two. But the same warning, make sure they are choreographically appropriate.

Many beginners in their eagerness to get dancing use very exaggerated hand movements and body language which looks distinctly undignified and communicates nothing to the dog except that you look like a Twinkie on speed when the music starts.

No wonder the dogs come to a stand still.

Awesome.

In addition to remembering the words, you will have remember that the left and right cues are FOR THE DOG, not for you, so if you have taught left paw and right paw when the dog is by your side, when the dog is facing you the cues will be the opposite way around to your own left and right.

STANDARDS

All cues need to be taught to the highest level, dogs must be able to remember the "code", what hand for what leg etc, have no hesitation in responding, and always give their best.

LEARNING THE GAME

The dog will need to be up to speed with concentration skills, learning to listen and watch your hands and body ALL the time. This is your communication which to be effective needs to be spot on to the music.

You will train yourself to "think twirl" and give the cue as the music approaches the twirl section so that to the onlooker it looks like the dog is moving to the music. If your signal to twirl is obtrusive the move can be spoilt.

Practise your sessions to music. This will affect your body language more than you think, certainly enough for the dog to be aware. In addition if the music changes your mood, then this needs to be the mood you practise in. A jazzy piece may make your fingers snap, add an extra wiggle. Use this as a subtle colour to the cue signals. To practise "cold" and then expect performance to a "colourful" chore-ography can totally confuse the dog and cause shut down or non-stop barking.

We are also susceptible to conditioning. If during your 106 practise occasions you adopt the "mood" for your music, then when you hear this in ring it will trigger the same responses. So practise "full on" as much as you possible can, provided your "full on" does not distort or damage the quality of the moves.

For Kiwi, a very receptive and excitable nature, I practise the full-on signals in a very slow and carefully exagerated style to keep the excitement level under control. Once she is not over stimulated by snapping fingers and waving umbrellas I begin to speed up to the real rhythm gradually.

My CD player has a "repeat" option, I set this for one particular track to generally train during 4 or 5 repeats with one dog. I can see easily if that rhythm is going to suit that dog, or more precisely does the rhythm make me move in such a way that the dog can read me easily?

It also helps the dog get used to training in noisy situation, it encour-ages the eye concentration.

LISTEN TO MUSIC

There is never enough time in the day already, so make sure all driving time has music as well, vary the radio stations. I rummage through CDs bins at the supermarket for cheap CD's and have found some great tracks.

Have listen-in sessions with other enthusiasts, you may find a piece that exactly suits another dog.

Finding the right piece of music puts wings on the training. Training alone will not work, without the soul of the dance pulling it together it can look stiff and a series of disjointed tricks. Good choreographers can put something together to ANY piece of music. But the ONE piece that is right makes the whole picture come together, the balance, the variation, the timing and the dog's and your natural rhythm is highlighted by the music.

There is also an element of "personality" in here as well. It is harder to find the right piece when you are a starter since you have not yet learned the strategy for changing your moods and moves to suit the music. You need a piece to suit you. Certainly keep a note of your "one day ..." choices.

GET A VIDEO CAMCORDER

This is going to be your ally, your best friend and your most useful critique.

Watch yourself, how the two of you look together and learn to reshape the way you move, your balance, speed and poise. These small things make all the difference.

I set up the camcorder on the tripod or table, wide angle and ignore the watching eye. You need to see the shape of the moves as seen by the spectator, not just your imagined view.

PROPS

These can be a terrific boost to your performance, an extra realm to the moves, and a good way to help you add drama to a routine.

CANE

Excellent for the dog to circle, jump over. Carrying the cane will need to be practised. You need to make sure you look more like Fred Astaire than Fred The Shepherd.

Practise with something very light, make yourself carry the cane all day long so it becomes natural to handle it, plant it under your arm, signal with it.

I envy American children who regard marching bands and baton twirling as a normal entertainment. I struggle to twirl even a pencil!

Canes or batons also make excellent target sticks during a routine. They can cue the dog for particular moves, especially at a distance.

HOOP

Again it needs to be carried with comfort, but excellent for the dog to move through. It would always look good if you can interact with the hoop as well.

I have a prize for the first person who can send me a video of their dog weaving through a moving hoop - one that has been rolled away from the handler and is self returning with backspin. Hmmm...

On the same lines as hoops and canes anything that works in the gymnastic sense, ribbons and balls, just think how great a routine would look with a ribbon?

YOUR OWN FEET

Yep, they will need to learn where to go.

If you already have dance training of any sort, then you'll understand what you need to teach yourself. For those brand new to dance I can advise you to find a class, any sort of class, from line dancing to tango. It will teach you the discipline you need to manage yourself, hear the rhythm develop your sense of "where am I?" .

Not only are we expected to manage ourselves, remember the "dance", where you are in the ring, where the judges are, but also the entire routine, anticipate every cue that needs to be given to the dog and "smile". You ARE having fun!

When we started teaching the dogs movements we wasted so much time teaching overlapping or merged movements, or were not precise enough in our expectations. In hind sight we hadn't realised how many movements there were or that the dogs would be able, with the help of the clicker, to understand the difference between them.

For once I encourage you to browse right through the book and have a peek at what is ahead. Then come back and take time to think about what you want to teach, don't let it be fuzzy or ill-defined. Most of the moves are suitable for all types of dogs, and some especially individual to your dog, the limitation is on our imagination NOT on the dogs' capabilities.

Look through every section and plan to teach a handful of things well rather than a bit of everything that is not so good.

KEY TO THE SECTIONS

The elements for the dog are divided into three categories. We teach each of the elements separately then they can be merged together:

1. MOVEMENT & POSES
walk on, trot up, back up, rollover, spin, circle, side steps, beg, take a bow etc

2. LOCATIONS
by my side, in front, behind, at the distance

3. DIRECTION
face me, face out, walk towards, walk away, go left, go right

Each of these will be taught separately and can be merged into fantastic new behaviours:

MOVE / POSE	LOCATION	DIRECTION	
trot up	left side	forward	= heelwork
trot up	in front	forward	= following the dog
backing	in front	facing	= backaway
side steps	in front	go left	= line dancing, waltz, or polka

KEY TO SYMBOLS

The diagrams can give you an idea on the description of the movement or the way you can teach it. I thought long and hard about producing a video, but I opted out since I believe that you can develop your own dog's style of the movement in your own interpretation rather than copy what you see is another dog/handler's interpretation. This is a very individual activity.

location = where the dog is relative to you

position = the position the dog is holding, ie the "pose"

hot spot = the place where the dog gets the reward

a dog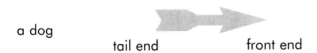

tail end   front end

a person

who has a front, a direction to face

If the dog is at heel or side position the side you have in common is the "inside" and the side furthest away the "offside".

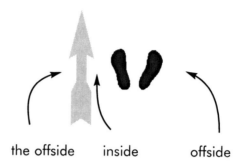

the offside   inside   offside

CLICKER FOR DANCE TRAINING

The majority of the learning in Dances we will be expecting movements from the dog. If you are not a moving type of person yourself, you may find the dog will not freely suggest a "move". Loosen up, be moving all the time as you cue, as you deliver the food, as you collect more food. The more animation you enjoy the more movement you will stimulate in the dog, the more opportunity to click and capture.

Clicker training in the context of dance movements is about capturing lured or stimulated behaviours rather than free shaping, which is excellent for the poses.

CLICKER GIFTS

Clicker training brings two particular gifts to Dances:

Firstly, being able to reward the dog's memory skills as they connect the cue you give with the move they do, without errrm .... "wassa a spin?". No hesitation, accurate responses. By allowing the dog to make their own connection between moves you have lured or shaped, and the cues you give will mean far less time practising by association, ie giving the cue AS the dog does the move.

Secondly the clicker allows you to spell out for the dog the precision of the movement you want, are the feet high or low in the "walk tall"? Is this a walking circle or a tight spinning top?

This bring hundreds of shapes to the choreographic "drawing board". To allow a combination of person, dog and music making a three way partnership.

Pay particular attention to adding cues and then practising cue recognition. Fast and accurate responses to minimum cues bring the dance alive.

Open your mind to the differences in the movements, be particular and exacting and you will have a great range to dance to and a dog with confidence that comes from clarity.

TARGET STICKS

For small or big dogs your target stick will become an essential tool. It allows you to keep your self upright with minimal body language and still move the dog though a extensive range of moves and shapes.

I use a telescopic stick that can stretches up to 4 feet and can be reduced as I wish to fade it. The dog's nose follows the end of a stick and the direction, speed and dimension (high and low) can all be cued with the minimal movement from you.

2 Key skills and movements

CONCENTRATION

RING STAMINA & FITNESS

FOUNDATION MOVES

CONCENTRATION

Concentration is a two fold job, not only does the dog need to be able to concentrate on the job and match the cues and signals to the right behaviours but also learn to shut out many distractions.

A dog with good concentration will:

Respond without hesitation

▶ this indicates the dog is focussed on you, it can respond to the signal or cue and carry out the action. If you can get top performance at home, but not in a new place, it is often a result of the dog's sense of security being diminished which has a knock on effect on their ability to concentrate.

Take no notice of surrounding distractions

▶ this sort of focus is easier to achieve with certain breeds, particularly stock working breeds, they need to be able to maintain visual contact with their stock, but ignore distractions such as pigeons or rabbits, or even in the case of my sheepdogs, trees! (We ran into the other sheepdog quite often as well).

▶ dogs that are outwardly focussed from their inherited behaviours, such as patrol dogs, or guard dogs, ignoring the circus around them can become quite stressful.

Maintain concentration with short breaks

▶ an experienced dog will be able to maintain concentration, This is not achievable in young dogs, and it requires the skill of the trainer to encourage concentration, always reward it, and let the dog build up concentration "stamina".

RECIPE 1 - CONCENTRATION

With titbit pot in hand or nearby, clicker at the ready you are going to teach your dog get a reward for focusing on you.

1. Throw several pieces of food on the floor, let the dog hunt around, as it eats each one, click.

2. After this food has all run out, the dog will look at you in expectation, click and throw the reward to the floor.

3. Gradually increase the criteria by throwing the food further away or behind you, and only click for the dog returning to the front of you. We call this "in front" and it will become the default position.

4. The first cue for In Front will be the way you hold your hands. Keep them in front of you as if you are holding a bird, something "secret". It may even be the food, but do not use the presence of the food as a lure.

This is one of our early conditioning exercises, and a good opener for all lessons, it is especially useful to get a dog familiar with new surroundings with low expectations. If a dog found this difficult to do then higher expectations can be forgotten.

Do not worry about the dog becoming a ground sniffer, you will move on from this. The dog will leave the ground and focus on you because YOU will be more rewarding. Preventing the dog from ground sniffing does not teach not to sniff around. But rewarding the behaviour of leaving the floor and seeking your eye contact is critical and should be practised regularly.

To encourage behaviours full of movement, some distance between the reward and the behaviour encourages more animation. Feeding direct to the stationery dog inhibits movement.

Racing to the food station, dropping food into a bowl, then racing back to your training area really zips the dog up.

To encourage focus you need to reflect focus back to the dog. Hold yourself in "engaged" mode, this is the greatest cue you can give. Do not be tempted with vocal cues like "watch me" or "pay attention". Both of these things are integral with every piece of learning and interaction.

This is often where beginner handlers fall down, they use a different body language when stressed or being watched and the dog is not "cued" to focus.

This is a wonderful game for all dogs, especially useful prior to performance, a nice "tune in" and interactive game.

As time goes by make the focal point harder to find, we call it "toffee to a blanket" training. After a while when you have cupped hands you will not be able to get away from your dog. The learning is then ready to be transferred to more difficult situations.

SENSE OF PERFORMANCE

Nearly all my new clicker training groups find that they can get good results at home but the standard is considerably lower when in front of an audience or class mate. Which is of course when you need that "sense of performance" from the dog and that extra effort!

This can be down to two things:

> ▶ what you consider "good" at home is insufficient. You can only learn what is sufficient from experience or inviting yourself to tea with a top handler and watching their "home" standards.

> ▶ the dog is experiencing stress in the performance environment which lowers standards. Stress can come from the speakers, the others dogs, the audience or the atmosphere.

It is a fairly accurate barometer of how a dog is "feeling" by the way they respond to you, the quality of their work and standard of the results.

This will not improve until the dog is not stressed in the performance environments. All the training in the world at home will not put a stressed dog into first place if the dog cannot cope with the stress.

Give your dog positive experiences in as many rich and new environments as you can find. Mix with lots of different types of people, scents, noises, other dogs.

Travel the dog widely and without expectation. Do not try to train in new places unless the dog clearly looks bored and indicates they are "up for it".

For many years my dogs only trained in the absolute quiet and peace of Welsh hillsides, never in class and never in towns or parks. They happily transferred their learning to shows and rings with no decrease in quality. They were exposed to a very rich environment of the sheep all around them, regular travel to supermarkets to wait in the car and always trained with their pack members nearby.

They were very skilled at coping with external distractions, of a particular kind, but they demonstrated they were able to transfer these skills to other weird and wonderful places.

RECIPE 2 CONDITIONING FOR PERFORMANCE

Dogs will become conditioned to their environment very quickly, this can be used to your advantage.

If a dog is surrounded by the performing "circus" and spends most of the time watching the entertainment then you are making it far harder for the dog to ignore this in the future.

Instead take your focus exercises, into an area near the "circus" and condition your dog that in these circumstances you will play the BEST games, give the dog the BEST motivation to focus on you, and that is focusing on the dog yourself. This is highly motivating for a dog to have you fully engaged.

This is also good for your concentratio as well. Very often we are not ourselves in the performance environment. We become self conscious and hyper sensitised to being watched. This is an alert flag to the dog and may even be the sole reason for the dog's stress. Practise the concentration yourself. Start in a quiet corner and put all your focus into the dog, exclude the other people until you feel you and the dog are in your own space and the feeling is the same good feeling that you get between you at home.

Use the distractions to your benefit not to your disadvantage.

In addition to reducing stress any performance animal can come alive if they have the right support in that environment. Some rare animals are born with a switch that flicks on when they feel the audience atmosphere. Others need to be made to feel they are a star. So careful think about how you handle this "protege" in the performance environment.

An anxious skater or athelete is not going to perform their best if their partner is not in harmony - this works both ways. The dogs need your support of them, especially in the early days, and they will give back ten fold what you invest.

PHYSICAL FITNESS

This will develop a lot from your training, particular movements for some dogs may seem clumsy in the early stages. So look and make the effort to train these movements to increase their agility and suppleness.

RECIPE 3 DEVELOPING PHYSICAL SKILLS

Each dog will benefit from its own programme of physical development. But you are looking for a dog:

▶ with an easily sustained trotting action, so plenty of road walk at the trot to strengthen feet and lower legs.

▶ able to maintain poised head carriage, even if the head if not fully raised, it will still be "collected" (as in horses), so plenty of neck strengthening exercises by playing tug games

▶ flexibility of the spine, for turns and moves, from teaching the dog to turn in tight circles

▶ lightness of foot for jumps, side steps, marching which can be developed from a modest amount of careful agility training

Even after my dog has learned the movement, such as a spin or turn. I will include a lesson about once every 10 sessions that reverts back to luring. This triggers "bigger and better" from the dog. That more fluent circle in the spin, an extra flexibility to the spine, a faster dive under the leg for the weave. This may not be the required type of movement, but encouraging an over and above the norm adds more physical strength. These are particularly useful to warm a dog up for each session, and after a longer break.

RECIPE 4 DEVELOPING MENTAL STAMINA

A performance can sometime last 3-4 minutes. The dog will be expected to maintain concentration, carry out 30 plus behaviours, sometimes repeat themall for no immediate reward.

Collies, bless them, often get their reward from the action and the working aspect. The collie "works" their partner. Looking for the signals are an intricate part of their make up. In sheep they look for that change in balance that indicates "this ol'ewe is planning to take off". They look for the flock veering off course when approaching a dip or shadow under trees. This is what powers their motivation and desire to keep in control.

Once the dance movements are learned, they take the place of the flanking movements and the collies are able to work through complex routines without any obvious reward.

Many other breeds were not installed with this chip!

When all the movements have been taught, they are reliable and robust, I introduce some mental stamina training.

This is aiming to give the dog more reserves to keep going for longer because the reward WILL arrive - outside the ring in the shape of a pheasant in Arnold's dreams!

I will plan to train for an intense 10 minutes. As the dog comes to the training zones they are full of energy and motivation. Whilst that energy lasts I train for verbal feedback. When that energy begins to subside I bring in a piece of foodfor every 4/5 behaviour. When the energy flags again I bring in the food for every behaviour. When the energy goes down again I carry the food in my hand. Finally I finish with a tremendous game.

The whole session may only last 3 minutes for a young dog new to training. It may only include 3 behaviours and all its variations. But the extra effort required as the dog is physically and mentally starting the flag is rewarded by greater or more frequent rewards.

In time each energy level will last longer. When the opening energy lasts for about 3 minutes you can think about a live performance. To do so before the dog can perform without reward for that length of time can inject some serious de-motivation into the ring situation.

Ideally all early performances should follow the increasing reward strategy. This is not always viable in competitions where toys and food are not allowed. Search out situations where you can perform without competition. Demonstrations are ideal and a great training ground.

FOUNDATION MOVES

Certain movements do not fit into any particular category, in fact they fit into all categories, so rather than send you backwards and forwards through the book I have put them here.

RECIPE 5 DON'T MOVE !

This is an essential move, possibly of limited use in the performance but immeasurable move in the training.

Most performances begin and end with an opening "pose". The dog is in a position, that may be tricky to sustain, and you need to keep it there until the point of the music starts your routine. Also you need to consider that this star child is going to be photographed "in the pose" so to speak, when they are famous!

During training, I often need to move myself to a particular position relative to the dog so that I can extend or add variation to a move. Without a "stay there" it becomes tricky to set up the situation.

Most of our training is for movement is usually started in the standing position. But teaching "don't move" is best done in the sit. You can utilise the learning for any position - the stand still, the beg "hold it", the roll "play dead". It can freeze an action part way through or immobilise a dog whilst you move instead.

The "stay still" learning

> ▶ The dog needs to develop the skill of not wanting to move, without any fear of moving. Therefore teach the dog that resisting movement is rewardable.

> ▶ Start from the sit and gently, very gently, push the dog from behind, you will feel their back muscles tighten up, click straight away. Over a couple of minutes you feel the dog strengthen those muscles and refuse to be moved. They want their titbit!

> ▶ Make sure the clicker is nowhere near the dog's head for this exercise or use a quieter clicker.

> ▶ As soon as they have learned resistance from pushing their back, gently tip sideways at the shoulder. You will end up with a rock solid sitter.

> ▶ Begin to add the cue as you feel the dog resist when you go to place your hand, anticipation is the indication of the dog's understanding of what is to come ... link that understanding then with the "freeze" cue.

> ▶ I use "stop".

RECIPE 6 STAY OUT THERE

Second stage is to teach the dog that being away from you is a rewardable hot spot (ie great place to be, since food rains from heaven).

▶ Ask the dog to do anything straight forward - like standing and looking at you, but engineer the reward to be sent beyond the dog. Be careful the dog doesn't try to jump for the food, twisting can cause injury.

▶ Start with the dog looking at you, click and throw the food beyond.

▶ Before the dog has had time to return close to you, click and throw beyond again

▶ After a few of these the dog gets the plot, eats, and stays where it is.

▶ At this point add your "don't move" cue

The point of this is to explain to the dog that not everything is carried out close by, it gives confidence to be at the distance which is essential when you want to move the dog out there, and this adds more variety to your routines.

RECIPE 7 SHIFT YER ARSE

If you've ever lived with big dogs - ie bigger that mediums! Then this will be an ingrained piece of learning other wise the day is spent kneeing the dog out of the way.

I firmly believe the Gordons have no awareness that they exist anywhere beyond mouth, nose, front feet and genitals. The rest is left to luck to sort out. So it became essential that if they were going to become Gay Gordons they had to learn they had a back end and learn how to manage it.

ISOLATE THE MOVEMENT

I start most of the puppy or first learning sessions with the concentration training turning it into a game. Whilst I am doing this I practice placing myself behind the dog so that they have to turn around to look at me to get their click and reward.

If you carefully plan this you can stand at such a point that only their back end has to move to be able to face me.

I start with the dog standing still "in front" and move to their shoulder with the food. Imagine there is a pole straight down through the dog's shoulder - rather like a merry-go-round horse, and you are looking for the dog rotating around this point.

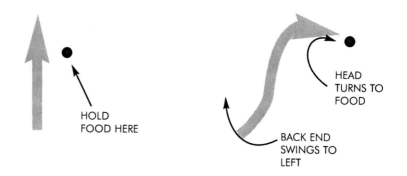

HOLD FOOD HERE

HEAD TURNS TO FOOD

BACK END SWINGS TO LEFT

If you take the head to one side, then the back end has to move, this is the move I click for - that single side step with one back leg.

Build up on this until the dog can rotate through quarter of an hour (if a complete rotation is 60 minutes on a clock). Make sure you teach both stepping to the left and the right.

This move does not have a cue, it is just a way of stepping for the dog to get to a certain point the shortest way. It will be incorporated into several specific movements.

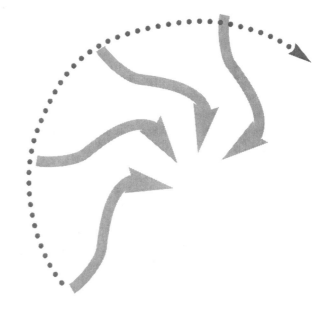

3 Location

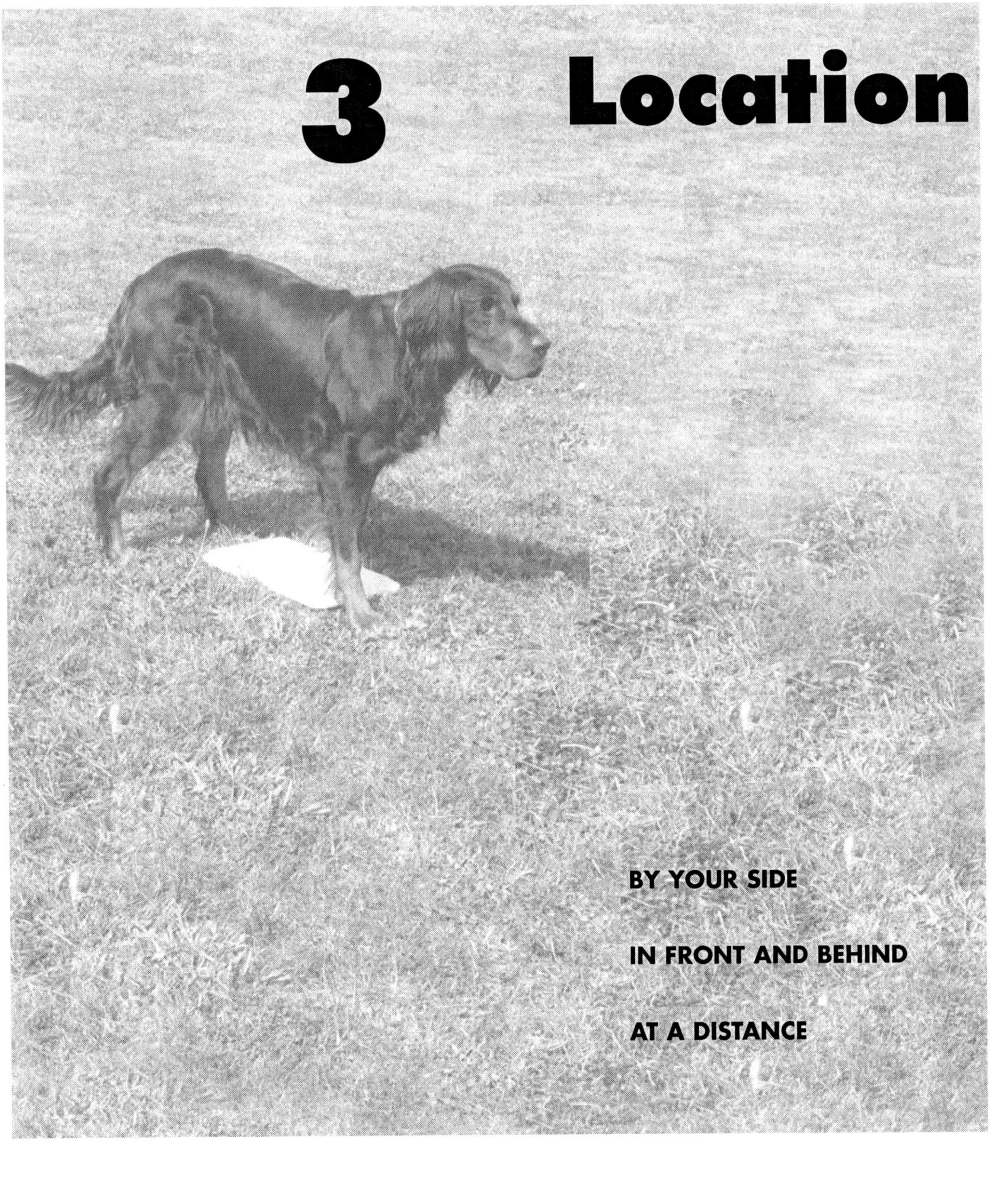

BY YOUR SIDE

IN FRONT AND BEHIND

AT A DISTANCE

There are four basic locations: **Cues:**   **How far away:**

on my left	close or here	zone 1	zone 2	zone 3
on my right	side or leg	zone 1	zone 2	zone 3
in front	front	zone 1	zone 2	zone 3
behind	be-hind	zone 1	zone 2	zone 3

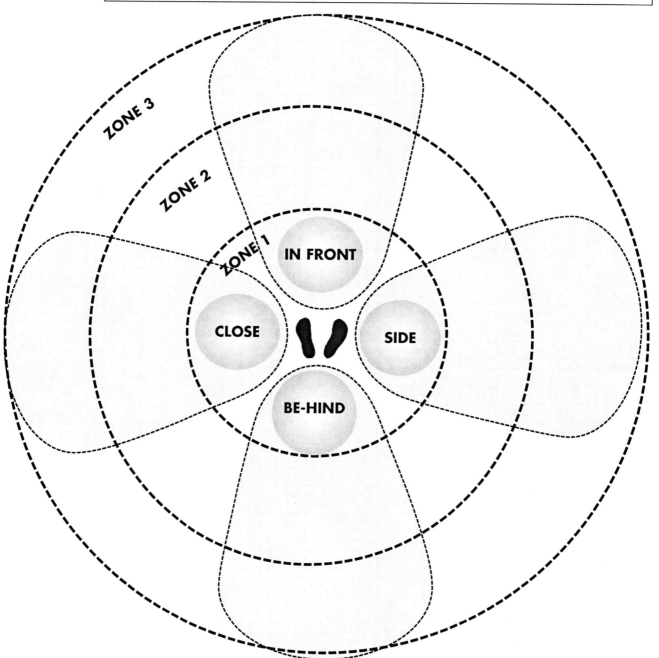

Do not set out to teach all locations. These will build as your repertoire increases. But if you plan at the beginning and label each location you will always be able to add more to the plan.

Start with: Front, zone 1
                     To your left, zone 1
                     Front, zone 2

It is important that you spell out to the dog exactly where the location is. Place the dog in a standing position and keep the dog in the location whilst you click and reward in the location.

(The correct location, the "hot spot", will be rewarded several hundred times so that is becomes a place the dog "lurves" to be. This applies to all locations, engineer a way to place the dog in location and thoroughly condition the dog this is an excellent place to be, and food will be delivered there.)

Engineering can be by luring or targeting the dog to a mat, and placing yourself in different locations relative to the dog, or using the wall or furniture to guide or box the dog in a stationary position.

RECIPE 8 LOCATION LEFT AND RIGHT HEEL

At the left or right side "close" & "leg", in zone 1.

This is the traditional heel location. I use food or touch back of hand to lure the dog to stand by my side with a wall or chair on the offside to prevent "flaring".

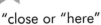

"close or "here"   "side or "leg"

Initially I lure the dog to the place with food, but then expect the dog drive upwards whilst standing to touch the back of my hand held about waist height for the Gordons, hip height for the collies. Just check your hand position is comfortable for the dog to reach and maintain focus on and that you do not pull the dog around the front of you. The heel location should be at your side, with room for you and the dog to show movement and balance. The power in this location is the drive upwards, the lift, not the lean on or contact.

Since Dances is all about movement, the sit becomes just a pose for a pause. Teaching a location to a sitting dog can inhibit movement so teach it in the standing position.

Once the dog is happy to maintain a location, ask for and reward several actions of head stretch to hand then you can begin to teach the dog how to get to a location.

MOVING TO LOCATION

For a dog to adopt a location it will need to be able to carry out particular moves. This learning will also help the dog to maintain the location whilst on the move.

BACKING INTO LOCATION

Whilst the dog in is location and you are rewarding with food, take a very, very small step backwards. The dog will now find your hands have disappeared slightly behind their head.

Keep the chair support to the off-side, and let the dog work out how to move back to the hot spot. Do not expect miracles, a movement of 6 inches is great achievement, and make sure you let the dog puzzle this out for themselves. It is VERY important they have the skills to stop themselves slipping out of position, going a bit to far forward as you walk can be avoided if the dog has learned how to pull back into the hot spot.

COMING UP TO LOCATION

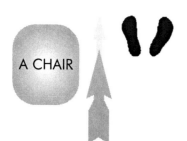

Taught similarly to the backing movement, just move yourself forward no further than the length of a shoe, keep your hands in the location and reward the dog when it comes forward for the touch again.

As soon as these movements are fluent and you can take a step forwards or backwards and the dog begins to anticipate your action, then add the cue prior to movement.

COMING TO LOCATION WITH SIDE STEPS

This is the same movement as side stepping which I have explained the beginnings of in the Foundation Moves (page 25). It is a great exercise to teach the dog to close in and adds mobility to their feet.

Once you have isolated the movement of stepping sideways with the back feet, move around the chair and as the dog joins you the chair will encourage their back feet to move into position. Click this precise movement and put on cue.

Once they can manage to side step the back end to location, then you can ask for a small side step of both front and back end at the same time.

Go back to the wall, move off the dog to the side only the length of your shoe and let the dog solve the puzzle.

Now we have equipped the dog with the skills to "get to the location". Check the learning by asking the dog to move to the location from further away. The dog should be able to come in from any angle.

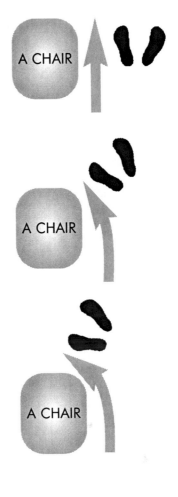

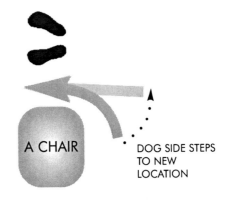

DOG SIDE STEPS TO NEW LOCATION

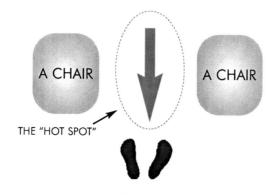

THE "HOT SPOT"

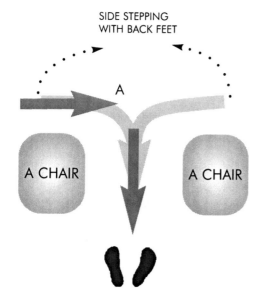

SIDE STEPPING
WITH BACK FEET

A

CLICK FOR
THAT
MOVEMENT

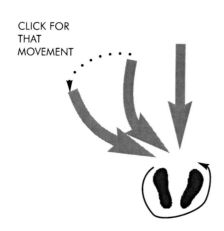

RECIPE 9 TEACHING IN FRONT

The dog will stand square in front of you, probably half their body length away. If they are too close as you both walk forward or backwards you will find you trip up on each other's feet and that extra bit of distance will give the dog a clearer view of your signals. You are more likely to stand up like a normal person, not crouch over the dog.

Teach this similarly to the side and heel location, firstly establish is as a "hot spot", possible a couple of chairs to keep the dog straight and square. Don't crowd the dog with the furniture and use the same technique to teach the dog stepping forward to location.

Using the lure, start with the dog at point A, step back between the chairs and draw the dog to follow you. As soon as you see their hind legs step to their left, click. It is the ACTION of straightening up that we now click, not the end position. Feed in the end position. Double rewards! One click for the correct movement and seconds later a piece of food in the right place.

Teach both sides. Usually they are more agile on one direction, but keep up the "Shift Yer Aare" exercises in the direction needing the greater mobility.

Once they can move the rear end across the front end and rear end moving simultaneously is far easier.

Teaching the dog to find the location is very similar to the foundation move of rotate, the side stepping of the back end, except this time the front end will need to side step as well.

RECIPE 10 SWING THOSE HIPS

This is an excellent exercise that will give you a great range of move and enhance the default "dance" position where the dog stands directly in front and facing you.

Standing on the spot you are going to rotate in a circle. The dog will maintain their position relative to you "in front". Click and reward EVERY side stepping action of the dog's hips, feet in the straight and squared up location. You can get several points of reward around each circuit.

Expect the dog only to achieve "15 minutes" around the clock at the most to begin with. Reward lots of small achievements before moving onto to "30 minute" segments.

RECIPE 11 MAINTAINING IN FRONT ON THE MOVE IN A STRAIGHT LINE

Begin with rewarding the hip movements as in the Swing exercise and then move into a straight line.

You will find that once the hips begin moving freely the straight line is much easier to achieve.

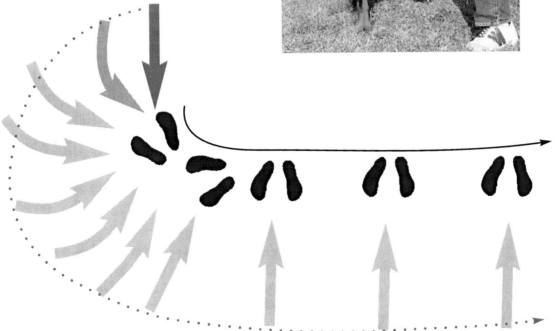

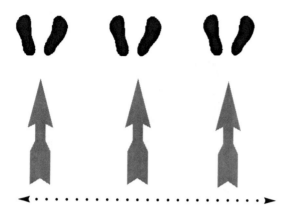

You can apply all the same principles to the "get behind" location - but you may need eye in the back of your head, a well placed mirror, or the French windows in the dark, to be able to see the dog's movement and success.

FACING WHICH WAY?

Once the dog is secure in the location you can use a change in direction to add more variety.

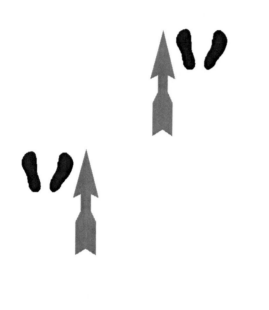

The dog can be In Front facing you or facing away. The dog can be in "close" but facing backwards instead of forwards.

For the change of side direction I bring the dog to location with the hand signal and use the verbal cue.

Now a tricky thing here. The cues can confuse some dogs BIG TIME. From their point of view, if they are on your left, with their right shoulder against you leg they are "close".

If they are on your right with their left shoulder against you they are "side".

BUT

If they are on your right, facing backwards, with their right shoulder against you, for some dogs this is the same as "close", ie they have learnt to make the contact point through the shoulder, and not relative to you.

Many dogs who have learned heelwork this way will easily swop to a right side facing backwards heel location very simply. You will just have to experiment and discover what the dog has actually learned ... which may not be the same thing as what you thought you have taught it.

RECIPE 12 FACING OUT

I begin this with teaching the dog to stand still, I walk around behind the dog, click and reward with food thrown outwards in front of the dog.

A target stick is extremely useful here. It gives the dog a focal point and they can line up their spine under the stick.

Take extra time here to establish it as a hot spot, the more advanced dogs will feel uncomfortable with their back towards you (can't check the signals, have to listen not watch), and the non-advanced dogs may see it as an excuse to go off shopping.

Once the dog is happy with me behind them. I stand at their side - with them across the front and ask them to finish the final steps to face outwards. "A"

From there start with them "in front" and let them complete the half turn outwards. "B"

This must be accompanied by a verbal signal, "Face out" since the dog can only listen, not watch.

MAINTAIN LOCATION

Once the dog understands the location you can have terrific fun placing the moves in all the locations.

The dog can back when in close, back when in front facing out as you walk backwards ... the only limitation will be your imagination.

CUES - SAVE YOUR VOICE

With all these locations once the dog has learned the location the dog can be expected to maintain the location relative to you. Initially the "maintain" it cue may be a hand signal but this can be dropped later.

Have the dog "in front" facing you. Walk backwards and the dog will stay "in front" and walk forwards towards you maintaining exactly the same distance and speed as you move. Once the dog has a good concept of "in front", we can begin many of the dance type of moves with our partner in the "dance" position.

If I move sideways so will the dog, just one cue "in front".

If rotate on the spot so the dog will rotate with me, just one cue "in front".

So you do not need to add the "movement" cue to get the action, but of course you must teach the dog how to move to maintain the location. Don't overload the dog with the extra cue of the movement, you can save this for when you have no body movement or you are moving in the opposite way to the dog.

So if Kiwi is "in front", and I walk forwards, she will walk backwards my cue is still "in front", not Back Up - that would separate her from me. I would use that cue if we were both walking backwards away from each other.

It may take a bit of extra training for the dog to grasp this, but better than having to constantly cue the dog during the action - your body language is ALWAYS the strongest cue. A simple hand to indicate the position for a young dog is a good, clear cue.

You can get some imaginative movements by simply asking the dog to change location. From left side to In Front to right side can give a great flared swing. From left side forwards to right side backwards (you change as well) can look like the Gay Gordon movement

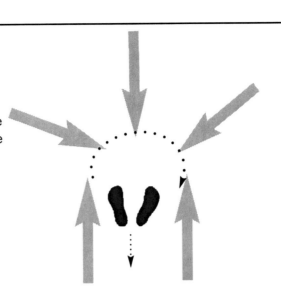

Walk with the dog right side, then ask the dog rotate to their left, instead of standing still turn right half a circle yourself and walk backwards with the dog now on your left.

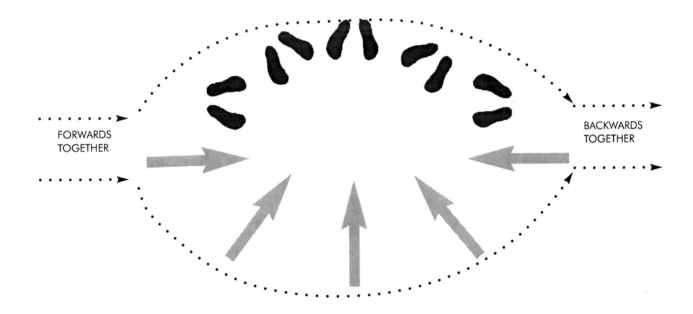

FORWARDS TOGETHER

BACKWARDS TOGETHER

4 Dressage Steps

FORWARD STEPS

BACKWARD STEPS

SIDE STEPS

We can teach the dog many movements with their feet - and every dog will carry out those movements within their own individual style. Train your eye to look for the natural movements of the dog through the day. Some forward actions of your dog will look more graceful and balanced than others and with this game it is not about just "moving" the dog we have to consider what to movement looks like to the spectator:

> ▶   does the dog waddle when it walks?

> ▶   does the dog jig up and down when it trots?

> ▶   does the middle section seem to go the opposite way to the front and back?

Identifying and capturing each of the forward paces can be useful - even if just to be able to say "that looks awful … forget it."

WALK

A walk is slower than a trot the dog will often move both legs on the same side at the same time, or slightly out of sync, body is quite relaxed, and the head posture slack

Cue: **WALK-ON**

For some dogs all they do is "walk" for others a walk is a considerable difficulty. It can be used to add a change of pace to your routine, more dramatic effect.

Part way between the walk and the gait (the dog's version of the horse's trot) is a very unbalanced movement called "pacing". This is where the same side of the dog is moving together. Try it yourself, walk with your right arm and right leg going forward, then your left arm and left leg, build up a bit of speed and you will start to rock from side to side as you walk. It is exactly the same as for the dog, it tends to happen more in the short backed dogs.

So we look for "opposite corners" working together, or diagonals. Left arm, right leg etc. (See Kent on page 42 trotting on the diagonal) Dogs will tend to have learned to pace if the speed you have asked for is too fast for a walk but not fast enough for a gait. So breaking the dog from pacing to gaiting is usually a change up in gear.

Set the dog up to move out with other people and really study your dog's movement.

- ▶ How many paces does it take to complete a smooth curve without changing rhythm?

- ▶ Does the dog perk up the way they move in the company of other dogs?

PLAIN TROT

This is the same as a horse's trot. It is done "marathon runner" style, which covers ground as efficiently as possible, usually low head carriage and very rhythmic style if the ground is smooth. Some dogs will have quite a degree of "bounce" others will have a very smooth action depending on their conformation.

Cue: not really suitable, since it is quite a disengaged movement.

HEADS UP TROT

This is very "collected", the balance of the dog is back and the drive is from the rear end, the head carriage is high, neck tucked in, feet lifting higher than usual, the dog is full of "watch ME" attitude. This will not cover the ground as fast as the plain trotting - more time of the action is wasted in walking on air.

Cue: **TROT OR HEAD-SUP**

All dogs can do both styles, it is a question of encouraging and capturing the second style since it happens more rarely and is a stimulated reaction. It also will depend on the dog being fit to sustain it for a length of time. It is a very athletic movement, more eye catching and graceful than the plain trot and more useful to us as a movement.

RECIPE 13 CAPTURING THE COLLECTED GAIT

▶   Begin by walking yourself backwards at a sufficient speed so that the dog trots towards you.

▶   Click and reward the dog for breaking into the gait. Aim to perfect this so that the dog moves off from standing straight into the gait.

▶   Arrange the focus of the dog up towards your face as you move backwards, either use a toy, titbits or the target stick. Use a temporary cue, like a tongue click, or "hup-hup" to stimulate the gait rhythm.

Your timing will be critical. The action you are looking for is smooth, with the drive upwards. Initially the dog will find it quite a difficult position to maintain and you will have to set aside time to get the dog fit with lots of training on the end of a tug toy.

This movement is easier to capture if you start with the running backwards yourself, the dog will find it easier to focus on you. Once this action is easily cued then transfer it out to the side - either target stick or hand and the dog follows the target and maintains the gaiting heads up action.

For the larger breeds you will find it difficult building up enough speed in running backward and you can begin straight away with the target stick.

At this stage you will not make progress until you can pass the following tests:

▶ Take your dog out to one side and gait it around in a large circle without breaking the rhythm. (You stay on the inside of the circle)

▶ Move backwards with the dog gaiting on a signal in or on your left hand, keep the dog gaiting without any break but move yourself to the dog's right and both continue forwards

▶ Gait the dog out to your side and circle the dog away from you in rhythm, move yourself to make the shape good and smooth.

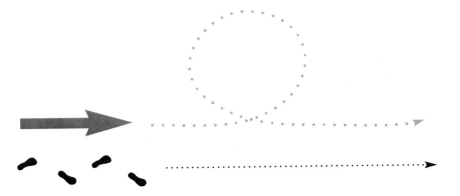

▶ Make the opposite movement where you turn the dog in a circle towards you

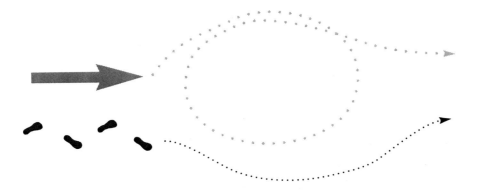

These exercises will teach you how to balance the dog whilst getting the dog gaiting fit, and the dog will learn to read your signals and anticipate the changes.

Once the dog is gaiting fit and you have the action or movement on cue, then you can add it to the location cues of either left and right side and you have instant heelwork!

RECIPE 14 CANTER RUN

This is the rocking action type of run, where the front legs of the dog both come up together and the back legs kick up together as well. If the dog is in first gear the front action will lead with one leg or the other on the down stride - which makes quite a pretty movement with some dogs. By fourth gear both legs are hitting the grounds together. Cantering is important with small dogs in routines. Exaggerating the pouncing action of the front end can make a new movement of its own.

Cue: FAST OR CANTER

You will need to be fairly fit to teach this to a medium or larger dog, running is essential I'm afraid.

Lift the dog with each bouncing stride. Think of using a target to encourage the slight lift the dog's natural collection of its front feet. It can be experimented with on the end of a toy if the dog will maintain a good grip.

Put the small rising "hup" on cue and match it to the dog's movement. You can easily do this with your stride in the heel or side location, where the dogs rises on each stride.

CONTROLLED STEPPING

Provided the dog has learned how to maintain a location these controlled slow steps are easy to achieve.

RECIPE 15 STALK

The dog will walk as if stalking with a low body carriage, very slowly with exaggerated pause between each stride of the front leg.

Cue: **STEP ON**

Take only one step at a time and signal the dog to walk on. Click and reward on every stride, feed the dog in position and the dog will soon slow down the movements waiting for their reward.

RECIPE 16 GOOSE STEP

With the balance further back and the legs reaching high in the air like a paw wave.

Cue: **KICK**

It is great to see this on a verbal cue, so that you can walk the dog step by step without moving yourself, good for dramatic effect.

Great for either the side location or in front as you walk backwards.

I add an extra diagonal movement for this so the dog looks like it is stepping out to each side as they cross their feet over.

Your left foot matches their right paw with the dog facing you in front. I then kick the left foot at knee height in front of my right knee. The move you exaggerate the side to side swing the more effective.

RECIPE 17 WALKING ON THE SPOT

This action of marking time can be taught by asking the dog to walk but restricting its ground coverage, or by asking for each paw individually. You will need to observe you dog's natural way of moving. To be as easy as possible for the dog the front feet will need to curl up under the dog not kick forward.

Cue: **MARCH**

This is one of those actions that requires you to experiment, for my dogs I ask them to walk backwards when they are standing in front of a wall, this cause them to dither which is the openings of the march on the spot.

I can also get the move by asking for very small alternating side ways moves until the dog is hardly moving at all. The click is critical to capture the rocking action.

Be careful of teaching it as a paw wave exercise as the back end may not move at all.

BACKING

Most dogs can move backwards equal to a trot speed. A confident dog will move faster if there is no fear of walking backwards into an obstacle. Some will virtually trot backwards with quite high stepping action, some will bounce backwards and some seem drop slightly and push themselves backwards.

Cue: **GO BACK**
BACK UP
WALK BACK

It is important that you teach this with a good "topline" on the dog. Dogs that have been taught to back by being crowded or pushed backwards will often move with the balance at their shoulders. This looks like the power for moving backwards is avoidance and gives a humped back appearance.

Clean walking backward dogs will have their heads raised and pull from their back end, with good level topline.

A "clean" back-walking. Head raised, point of balance further back

The direction the dog is moving in affects the shape of the action - whatever the dog is focusing on will affect the way it moves:

▶ Heel or side position, the dog will be focusing on maintaining a position relative to you. This can often cause them to flare as they back, so their concentration will be focused on keeping the rear end in position, avoiding going under your feet and at the same time looking at you out of the top of their head!

▶ Backing away from you, is a good relaxed move, particularly if the dog is heading towards the reward point, they can't seem to whiz fast enough!

▶ Backing from a distance towards you, ie backside first. This comes in all shapes and sizes. Some dogs are quite happy to rely on you being where you say you are and will trundle backwards by ear radar, others will need to scrunch themselves up and look for you out of the top of their head or from side to side as they move. Surprising I've not see a dog walk backwards as we would, looking over your shoulder.

In fact dogs are a LOT better at going backwards than we are.

TEACHING WALKING BACKWARDS

There are two parts of this exercise - getting the movement and getting the direction.

The dog must be able to back with confidence. Begin by teaching the dog HOW to step backwards by staying with the dog every step. Your choice is between the dog to side or heel, or the dog in front.

RECIPE 18 BACKING IN FRONT

This is good for dogs not familiar with holding a tight heel position. Place the dog within a channel - something you can both comfortably walk backwards and forwards in:

The first and hardest piece of this exercise is the first step backwards. Most dogs know how to get out of your way, but if you push against them, or simply crowd them they will often move to one side, NOT backwards in a straight line hence the channel.

Click for all backwards movement, just the first step. Judiciously place rewards on the floor between your feet and then stand up straight and you will find the dog naturally "backs-up" after eating to see your hands and face again - good start.

If the dog makes like a lump of wood, you can use your target to indicate to the dog how to move backwards. Do not try too fast too soon, this is not an exercise where anxiety should be introduced.

RECIPE 19 BACKING TO A TARGET

Excellent choice for a dog used to targeting to a mat and if you are good with your timing. Start, sitting comfortably of course, with the dog happily standing on their mat. Lots of reinforcement that standing "here" gets food, it is the hot spot.

Then place a couple of objects in front of the mat, like cones to make a gate way. In fact we call this "parking the dog in the garage"!

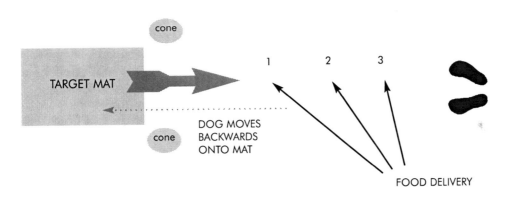

Initially when the dog is standing on the mat, facing forward out of the gateway click and reward. Place the reward between the two gate posts objects. Design it so that the dog comes forward no more than half their body length off the mat.

Then just sit tight, the dog will want to move back to their mat. Only click when all feet have arrived.

The cones will channel the dog backwards in a straight line. As the dog gets more fluent, place the reward closer to you (3), further away from the mat. Before long they will be chugging back into the garage like Thomas the Tank Engine!

When you are ready to increase distance, do not move the mat further away, move the food and yourself further away.

RECIPE 20 IN THE SIDE OR HEEL LOCATION

This is good for confident heel working dogs and a great exercise to enhance the heelwork. Start with the dog by your side and a channel or guide on the offside to keep the dog in a straight line.

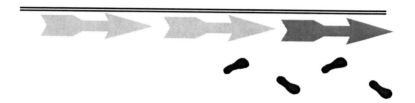

You will need to be able to use the lure with care, since raising the target over the dog's head will encourage them to sit. I begin this with the dog in the standing position and take my hands, food and body backwards no more than half the body length of the dog. If you are close enough to the wall the dog will not be able to come around the front to face you, but choose to back up to get a good view of everything. Again start with small steps.

If the dog is a confirmed sitter in this position, start in the stand and place the lure on their chest.

The aim of these exercises is to give the dog fluency in the movement. I expect if I asked you to trot backwards you'd be complaining how your legs hurt, or you "cant' go faster" quite quickly, it just takes practice.

Before you move on to teaching advanced backing the dog MUST be confident backing in all of the above situations, the more you transfer the learning and skills to different situation the stronger the learning and capabilities will become.

RECIPE 21 BACKING IN HEELWORK

After you have a confident dog and you can trot backwards yourself you can start to do this together.

The greatest room for error will be the dog not maintaining a straight line. They will tend to keep the shoulder in contact with the heel location, but the backend will often flare out. Equally if you over work this backend staying in a straight line the dog can over compensate and get under your feet.

the dog "flaring" out   the dog over compensating

I usually only incorporate and only practice walking backwards in a dead straight line, keeping myself very square and facing forwards. Mirrors are excellent for this training. Practice a good speed in this as well, it looks very effective and you will discover that dogs can go back faster than we can.

Transfer this to both sides of heelwork, it is excellent for consolidating the learning, and also transfer it to In Front and Be-hind. The same exercise but just a different location, the dog will not be cued to "go back" just "in front" and your movement is mirrored by the dog.

Pay attention to only click when the dog is in a straight position AND moving.

RECIPE 22 BACKING OFF

So far we have looked at training the dog to back in partnership, mirroring our movements. Great to incorporate into a routine, but dogs are such great backing machines and this presents a whole variety of moves and actions once they are confident.

The best exercise for teaching the dog to back off alone is the parking in the garage. It gives the dog confidence to have a place to "back to", a goal.

I have also used the change of floor surface as the "goal", in a hall, carpeted at one end, and the dogs back until they go over the carpet edge. Even quite anxious dogs like this sense of purpose.

Once the dog is backing confidently back to their mat, they do not need you to accompany them, and you can even go backwards yourself away from the dog then you can remove the mat and work on the action, not the target training. (But don't hesitate to bring back the mat if the exercise deteriorates)

DEADLY SINS OF BACKING TRAINING

▶   Clicking when the dog stops

This will teach the dog to stop to get the food, backing is about movement

▶   Saying "back, back, back, get back, back off, go back" just to get three steps

Discipline yourself, if you don't make the first error, then this is less likely to occur. Just one cue, one continuous movement, click on moving.

▶   Trying to get too long a distance to start with

Made ground slowly, place a mark for yourself on the floor, always click when the dog goes over the mark, take a small step backwards yourself to increase the distance.

▶   Backing the dog towards insecurity

The dog will need to trust you that they are not going to walk into furniture, people, other dogs or anything that will make them anxious.

▶   Using a hand signal

This is one for the voice only, backing alone can be done from every position, so keep it hands free.

RECIPE 23 BACKING TOWARDS YOU

Cute, huh?

Dog walks backwards away from you, turns around and walks backward towards you. Really cool exercise bordering on the inelegant!

Teach this as the "park the dog in the garage" in the earlier exercise. When I taught this the "garage" was through my legs. What a mistake!

You end up with the dogs klonking into your shins, you look like a break dancer on speed trying to move the "goal posts" to catch the dog, who is travelling very fast and only looking out of the back of their head.

After I gave more thought, I began training back in the channel with a small table for a reward point at the front. Click when the dog is flowing well and reward from the table.

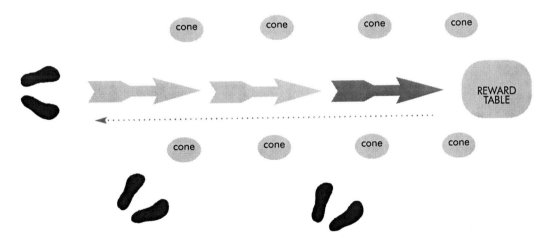

Connecting the back off (going alone backwards away from you) to the back towards you with a turn is best done after you have taught the dog backwards weaving and circles.

SIDE STEPPING

Without forward or backward progress the dog will move to the left or right, with both front and back assembly moving together and the spine staying straight. Just as we move sideways by either crossing one leg over the other to cover the ground or step out to the side and close one leg up to the other, so do the dogs.

Cue: **HAAAR** dog left stepping
GEEE dog right stepping

Remember this is the direction of the dog's leading legs, not necessarily your direction

Factors for the dog that influence their move are usually based in the should assembly and width of chest, as our is often affected by the width of our thighs [cough], but when done elegantly this is a very pretty move for the small stepping dog and with a larger stepping dog looks really neat if both handler and dog match pace for pace.

The key to the move is the importance of the dog staying parallel as it moves:

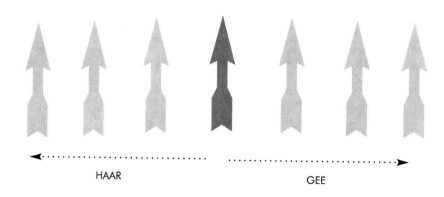

HAAR   GEE

You can place yourself in any one of the locations relative to the dog. In Front, Behind, to the left and to the right Heel position.

For an inexperienced dog you can move together and mirror the move, for the more experienced you can move separately to contrast the move. So planning for that eventuality means these directions will have verbal cues as well as "maintain location" non cues.

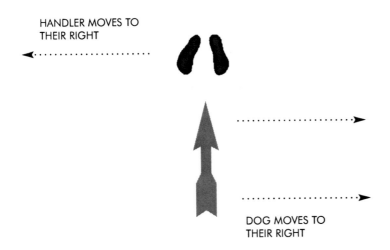

HANDLER MOVES TO
THEIR RIGHT

DOG MOVES TO
THEIR RIGHT

RECIPE 24 TEACHING SIDE STEPPING

Always the start point, teach the dog how to do the movement and gain fluency.

Re-read the section on teaching the side and heel position, this is the beginning of this move. The dog must have good awareness of their rear end and be able to side step with it, for warm up I start with a rotating circle. I often see this exercise fail because the handler continues the side stepping BEFORE the dog has completed and straightened up.

For dogs that find this movement uncomfortable or always seem to be late with the rear end movement carefully check to your timing.

Click when the dog initiates the **REAR END** movement, reward in the hot spot. Do not fall into the trap of flapping your hands around or twisting over to correct the dog, these signals become incorporated as cues and the dog will wait until the cues are given before movement.

You are looking for the dog to move both front and back assembly simultaneously. Take only one step at a time and do not continue the movement until the dog is setting off with simultaneous front and back leg movements.

The same applies to the In Front position. I tend to only teach the sideways move to heel as I am moving away from the dog, later on I will teach it with me stepping into the dog, but only when the dog is on verbal cue in that direction, I do not want to rely on knocking the dog to get the move.

You can experiment in front of a mirror to see whether you are better balanced and matching the dog whether you step off with the outside leg, or cross your inside leg over the other leg. If the dog is used to maintaining contact with the inside leg then this cue is logical for them. Quite frankly my thighs are too pudgy for that move!

You can also experiment with taking the cross over leg forwards in front of the other leg and then behind, I believe this is called the "vine" in line dancing, and it gives balance to the move, provided the dog is not surging backwards and forwards to keep the leg contact point.

ADDING VARIATION

If you dog can complete the move well it is worth exploring all variations:

> ▶ You can travel backwards and forwards whilst the dog travels sideways:

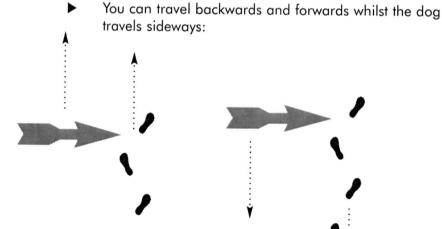

And of course the dog can move behind you as well.

CONTRASTING MOVEMENTS

Up to this point the dog has mimicked our movement, to be able to move separately we have to be able to cue the movement by signal but not move ourselves. If you have this level of achievement in mind move onto it fairly smartly, the longer you stay on mirrored moves the harder to break the association.

Go back to the target stick, it is especially useful to get the idea over the dog that movement sideways can be independent of me, so I teach the dog whilst I stand still.

I usually start with the dog in front, move with the dog a few steps in both directions but hold the the target lure in front of the dog. I point the lure the direction the dog moves in, keeping the stick horizontal and shortened.

From the dog's view:

go to your right - sideways   go to your left - sideways

Once the dog seems to be following the target stick I begin the move only for one step and take the aerial along to move the dog further on, flip the aerial around and bring the dog back to In Front, go a few steps the other way - keep the stick moving whilst I stay still, flip it around again and back the other way.

The dog is more likely to successfully continue a movement than start from cold if unsure. Click when the dog moves without you following only the target.

From there I will open the stick up to full length, stay still and move the dog from me, turn the stick, move the dog back to In Front, keep the momentum and move the dog out from me the other way.

This is using the stick as a temporary cue, once fluency is established then you can practice connecting the verbal cue with the moves until the stick is no longer required, which is easier to fade with a shrinking target!

5 Circles

CIRCLE, SPIN, ROTATE

SERPENTINE, WEAVING

REVERSE CIRCLES

**BACK OFF, REVERSE,
BACK TOWARDS YOU**

BACKWARDS WEAVING

Clearly identify in your own mind the difference between a "circle" and a "rotate" or "spin".

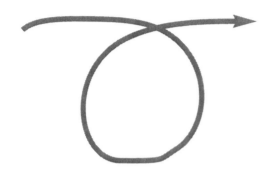

Essentially a "circle" is the pattern the dog walks, trots or gaits around. It can be any size from 3 feet in diameter to the width of the ring.

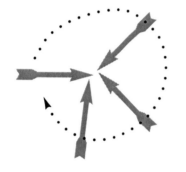

A "rotate" is where one part of the dog stays on the same spot and the rest of the body goes around, this will only ever be as large as the length of the dog's body.

The "spin" is where the dog turns very tightly on the spot and almost flips around in a turn.

At first it may seem that being particular about the movement the dog carries out is excessively fussy, but all these moves present a different shape to the spectator. They can be choreographed for different emphasis, a circle can be quite languid and leisurely, the rotate a very rhythmic stepping dance and the spin, fast and choppy to match the punctuation of the music.

It is certainly no problem for the dog to learn the differences between the moves, clicker training has opened up access to the dog's phenomenal memory and learning skills. I think they appreciate clarification on the movements, the same as when you ask for a sit, the dog needs to know "which sit ?".

CUES

Always use a different cue for each direction, clockwise and anticlockwise or right and left leading circle.

This is best cued with a word which allows for you to move separately from the dog. If you use a hand signal it can encourage the dog to jump in the move, which is not healthy, and can generate more speed than is good for the dog. Hand signals also encourage the dog to watch - but if the dog is turning away it can distort the circle trying to maintain visual contact. A dog will always do a better, healthier turn if its head is not abnormally raised.

Look for all spins, rotates and circles with all four feet on the floor. Leaping in a turn can be bad news for the health of the dog, particular if practiced repeatedly.

Some dogs will miss-shape the circle and tighten into a spin, so watch your timing with the clicker.

DOG HEARS
THE CLICK

The click will tend to "pull" the dog back to the point of reward. If you click when the dog is at the furthest point then it will cut the circle short and come direct across to you - almost in a "D" shape, not an "O". This is useful for spin training but not for circle training.

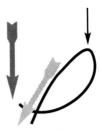

RECIPE 25 FREE CIRCLES

The dog completes a left or right circle, clockwise or anticlockwise in the location it is at and returns to the start point. The movement is a consistent gait, trot, walk or run.

Cue **CIRCLE** = Clockwise
A-ROUND = Anticlockwise

This is an excellent exercise for increasing the suppleness of the dog's spine. Always teach both directions even though you will find either you, or the dog, are more comfortable in one direction or the other.

Use the target stick for this, it ensures you get a smooth circle without contorting yourself. The hardest part for the dog to learn is the turning away from you. The target stick gets them over this initial hesitation.

GET A FLUENT SHAPE

Initially before the dog can learn this move for themselves, experiment with floating the dog around on the end of the target stick. See how you can draw shapes, take a note of the flexibility of the dog, some will jump and leap about - click only when they trot after the stick. Some will resemble a Land Rover towing a Caravan - back and front end working as separate vehicles with a tow bar between.

You need to become adept at maneuvering the body by remote control with your target stick. You only have control of the sharp end to lead by, but you must get a sense of the following bulk, how it will take short cuts, what happens if the target goes over the head.

Practice walking the dog around a series of figures of eight, some in front of you, some to the side and some going away and coming towards.

TEACH THE TURN OFF

The success of this exercise is made the minute the dog successfully carries out the "turn off". If the dog is standing facing you, provided you can teach the dog to walk away to the left or the right then the completion of the circle will follow.

This is the part to start to focus on teaching the dog. Use the target stick to commence the circle, click as the dog follows, complete the circle with the target and feed when the dog returns to "in front". The smart part is the turning away, by clicking at this point the movement will gain strength easily.

Work at this until the dog does not need more than one single gesture from the target stick to turn. If you have hesitation, or need to repeat the signal, stay at this point.

Be flexible and teach it in all positions you can reach. If you only teach the dog to circle In Front, then the dog will tend to return to this point, even if you initiated the circle in the heel position.

ADDING THE CUE

Begin with the dog In Front, before moving the target, give the verbal cue, then count 2 seconds, give the target signal:

1. dog stand In Front

2. give verbal "circle"

3. count 2 seconds

4. move target stick clockwise to move the dog's head

5. click on follow movement

6. feed when target led back to In Front.

Patience will pay off - you will need to wait for the dog to make the connection between the sound they hear ("circle") and the movement that follows. As always when adding cues, this is critically important - let the dog do the learning in their own way.

Remember to click when the dog makes the connection. For a few repetitions the circle may lose shape on that early click, but use the target to complete the circle and feed back In Front.

PRACTISING

The dog will need lots of practise, as will you, remembering which word is "go left" and which word is "go right". You can't do enough!

The key for success in moves where the dog can take a 50:50 chance in being right, is the first decision "is this to my left or my right?"

▶ If you find the dog difficult to move around in a circle start by just standing behind the dog, click when he looks at you, and feed when the dog arrives facing you.

▶ Sometimes, particularly long backed dogs, or dogs that back away when the target or hand goes over their head, it can seem very clumsy to get them to start the turn of the head. Begin your circle by bringing the dog close across the front and you will find their head turn easier to secure. (1, 2, 3)

RECIPE 26 GO AROUND

As for the Free Circle the movement is a consistent gait, trot, walk or run. Except in this case the dog will go around something specific. The dog can Go Around you at about 1-2 feet distance or around one leg or around a pole. It is the same movement, you only need to indicate to the dog "round what?" The dog can also be sent to 10 feet and told to go round.

Cue **CIRCLE** = clockwise
A-ROUND = anticlockwise

After teaching the dog the clear movement of walking around in a circle as opposed to spin on the spot, you can now attach the movement to a variety of objects. You will simply add the object cue in front of the cue for left circle or right circle:

"pole - circle"

"leg - around"

Or you can use the circling verbal cue in conjunction with a hand signal, to send the dog around you, or the pole etc. Once the dog has focused what they will be circling around you can continue with only the movement cue, not the object cue.

RECIPE 27 GIANT CIRCLES

For some breeds this can be their default behaviour - collies like to circle, the better to manage you by, and they often circle at a distance to have a better view of their sheep (you)!

Begin by teaching the dog to circle after they have learned to back to a good distance, perhaps 10 - 15 feet. Once they are aware of holding this distance you are only a small step away from adding the circular movement.

Be careful when you give the "circle or a-round" cue they do not get confused with "stay where you are and circle there". Start with the dog off the left side in a very large distance heel position (10 feet) until they get the idea, then gradually change this over into the "back off" - "circle-out" cue.

Remember that when you click at this distance the dog will hold the distance better if the reward is delivered at the distance also.

RECIPE 28 SPINS

Where the dog spins in a tight circle on the spot. The dog can also seem to "flip" this or spin around their centre of gravity. Movement will be to the left and right.

Cue: **TURN OR TWIST** Clockwise
SPIN OR TWIRL Anticlockwise
Don't use the combination of the similar sounding words, twist & twirl.

Spins and twists seem to be enjoyed by a great many dogs, without exception 100% of collies and some become so addicted that stopping the spin becomes more important, so beware of them going into spin overload!

Dogs can seem to turn one or two spins and be very aware of where they are, come out of the spin at the right point, but several spins will make the dog giddy.

Begin by luring the dog in small circles both to the left and the right, you won't need a clicker to start with, you are just warming up the muscles. Observe the shape the dog makes, how much their spin bends etc. If the dog is new to this move you will notice over time how much more flexible their spine becomes, so don't try to tighten them too much to start with, this will come with time, after exercise and understanding.

If you have a dog that resembles a log-with-legs begin by turning in small steps:

▶ Hold a titbit to the dog's nose and move yourself behind the dog whilst holding the titbit quite still. Then when you are ready just use the food to turn the dog towards you.

▶ Stand the dog across the front of you as close as you can get, again use the titbit to hold the dog still whilst you position yourself. Try to turn the dog "off" you, ie away from you.

▶ Make sure you manoeuvre the dog both ways, even though one way or the other will seem easier.

Words are cues are not relevant whilst you build up the flexibility - this may take a couple of weeks, plan some regular training every time you pop the kettle on and walk the dog around a couple of tight circles. Don't try to go faster or "wind" the dog up and be careful the dog does not start to jump in the movement, with a bent spine this can spell long term damage or pulled muscles.

Add the verbal cue when you can achieve with ease:

▶ the dog turns a full circle

▶ you can turn the dog both way with the same hand

▶ you don't have to bend over the dog or make like a windmill

then start to wean the dog off the hand signal and replace it with a verbal cue.

ADDING THE CUE

The long term cue for the move will be either a very subtle hand signal, but by choice a verbal cue. The dog will have a far greater repertoire if they can carry out this move in all locations, even when you are moving in a contrary direction.

- ▶ Take up the clicker, use the hand signal WITHOUT the food

- ▶ Click as the dog passes through the furthest point away from you

- ▶ Feed on arrival back in front, when the dog has completed the circle. Avoid feeding at an angle since the dog will learn to stop short.

As you click take your hand away so that the dog completes the circle "target-free".

For a while you are going to lose the shape of the circle, since we want to focus on the opening part of the move. All the early muscle warming will ensure that the dog will return to a well shaped circle once they have learned the cue and direction.

The hardest and most crucial part of the exercise is the first turn of the dog's head. They will be presented with a sound (your verbal cue) and they have to remember "is this left or is the right?"

Regard the dog standing in front of you facing you as at 6 o'clock, we will take the dog step by step round the clock through 9 o'clock, 12 o'clock, 3 o'clock and home to 6 o'clock. This is the clockwise turn, or "spin".

The routine will be to introduce the verbal cue and reduce the hand signal:

- ▶ give the verbal cue "spin", count 2 seconds:

- ▶ using the hand move the dog to 12 o'clock click and let the dog return home to 6 without hand signal. (2)

Remember with clicker training you don't have to worry about associating the word with the movement, just allow the dog time to build up the "sound" with the hint of the hand signal that follows. It is important they learn to work out which word is which direction themselves.

- ▶ repeat as above but start to reduce the hand so that is drops out earlier - about 9 o'clock. (3)

Stay at this point until you see the dog anticipating the movement from the 9 o'clock point.

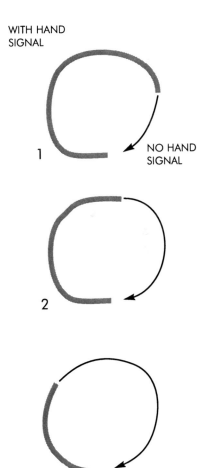

WITH HAND SIGNAL

1   NO HAND SIGNAL

2

3

Now we have a dog that hears the word, clearly and without hand signals distracting it from listening, and a dog that has shown that once you start off the spin they can complete the rest of the way by themselves. Just work on one direction until the cue is secure.

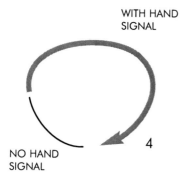

WITH HAND
SIGNAL

NO HAND
SIGNAL

4

▶ Trust your training. So far the dog has followed the hand signal, and now you are asking the dog to listen and recognise.

▶ Pay particular attention to the timing. You will give the signal, hold your hand in preparation to give the signal, and count to three. Give the dog a bit of "mental space" to make the connection.

▶ The minute the dog either turns their head towards 9 o'clock or take the first step. CLICK, get in there, let the dog know - "what a brilliant deduction ... you made the connection"

▶ The dog is very unlikely to complete the circle when they hear the click so early. No worry, just the next time after the dog has taken the step use the reward lure to complete the circle. (4)

▶ As soon as the dog has done this 2 or 3 times then withhold the click until it is further around the circle.

Remember that with clicker training we have two points of reward, two places we can say "well done".

The first is remembering the cue and starting the move, the second is completing the move. Once the dog can complete the move on verbal cue, don't go back to using the training hand signal.

With a verbal signal you can attach it to a variety of body movements. Remember Saturday Night Fever, with the finger pointing up to the sky on the hip swing - so just do the move and give the verbal cue.

You can spin and turn the dog on foot signals, which looks very effective if you cross your leg over the other and kick (not the dog), but the dog spins on the kick, step back change feet and turn the dog on the other leg kick.

RECIPE 29 ADVANCED CONTRARY CUES

Spins and turns are very much a part of dance moves and really add pace to a routine. But they can be more effective when both you and the dog turn together, but it has to look polished.

If you are walking side by side you can both turn in the same direction, but it looks effective if you turn in the opposite direction as well.

Before you start to confuse the dog by giving the cue then walking away ... "hey, what's going on?" check that the dog is up to standard by asking for a move at any position around you.

When I stand chopping up the titbits the dogs are usually somewhere behind me in the hopes for an over spill. This means they cannot stand in front of me, their usual place for a spin or turn, so I give the cue when they are behind, some just consider I've gone nuts, but what the heck we'll give it a try, and some consider a turn in that place and absolute no-no.

But this is an excellent measure of the dog's learning, and it generalises the movement, pushes it up a notch. A dog doing the spins anywhere but the usually spot gets a click and MAJOR reward.

Once the dog has fluency and spin at a distance, then teach the dog that you will cue the spin and turn your back.

Dogs are very self aware of where they are they often try to come back to where they were in relation to you, but since you are not where you were this starts confusion!

Focus the dog on the opening steps, throw the food away to avoid the dog trying to return to a spot no longer there or add another cue to locate the dog, "in front, side" etc.

RECIPE 30 HEELWORK SPINS

Asking a dog to leave the heel or side position for a spin is very effective when the timed to an emphasis in the music. Just take some time out to think about the spin and get the best from this move.

If the dog is level with you and you ask it to turn off go around and come back to the same position then the dog will be forced to catch up with you as you will have moved on from the original spot. This

can add quite a bit of stress for some dogs and even mis-shape the move in their effort not to be left behind.

But there are some alternatives:

TAKE A STEP BACK AND FORWARDS

This allows the dog to join you as you set off again. So the walk would go:

▶ with the dog in the left side heel location, as your right leg touches the ground, cue the dog to spin, do not put your full weight on your right leg

▶ put you weight back onto your left leg

▶ let the dog come in to join up with the left leg and both proceed forward together

TAKE A RIGHT TURN

Again if the dog is at your left side heel location as the dog turns off you make a right turn.

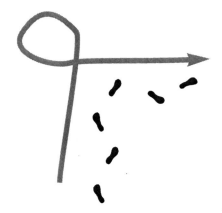

▶ Cue the spin on the right leg touching the floor

▶ with the left leg step back turn to your right

▶ set off with the dog on the left leg join up

COMBINATIONS

This is only limited by you imagination, there are some excellent combinations in the ring of weaves with a spin or turn on the outside, alternating spins and turns at the "in front" location as the handler travels backwards and forwards.

Very often the move can be used to simply face the dog a different way, and you "capture" the dog out of the turn to a new location - swapping sides and locations.

But for all spins and turns and any other move, once the dog is fluent and confident then they will offer these moves in the most unusual places!

RECIPE 31 ROTATE

The dog will move sideways whilst still facing the handler and complete a circle. The dog can either be in front or to heel or side, the handler can either stand still or turn on the spot. The rear end of the dog will take larger steps than the front end.

Cue: **THE LOCATION CUE** to maintain the position
SWING when carried out independent

This is an excellent exercise for teaching the dog greater mobility with their back end. You need to teach the foundation move Recipe 7 Shift Yer Arse to get the dog aware and in control of their rear. The dog will also need to be able to take side stepping action with their back legs.

The dogs learn to read your shoulder set for this, so pay attention to being "square" to the dog yourself, and they will know which goal posts to line up with, if you twist your shoulder to "square up" the dog this will not help.

USING THE MOVEMENT

START

I think this movement looks very elegant with the long back dogs that swing gracefully.

If the dog is in the heel or side position this is the "pivot" turn, when you rotate on the spot towards the dog, make this at least a half circle if not more, but always check you stay on the spot and DON'T walk around the dog

The dog can also learn to move this rotation independent, I start with the dog In Front, and whilst I stand still ask the dog to move to the left or right side through side stepping.

Just that movement alone looks very effective, and even more so if you turn to meet the dog.

▶   stand with the dog In Front

▶   cue the dog to the left side heel position with rotate

▶   turn yourself right a quarter of a turn as the dog moves

▶   you will both now be facing to the right of your original position

FINISH

RECIPE 32 SERPENTINES

The dog will trot, gait or walk in half or part circles alternating the direction of the curve. This is usually done free, off the handler, when done in the heel position the dog simply maintain position.

Cue: "**FOLLOW**" with the hand or pole as the target

The dog can serpentine across the front of you, when you are walking backwards or even walking forwards.

The amount and size of the half circle can open up a whole range of very interesting moves. The dog can go through a "shallow" serpentine walking fairly fast following the handler who is walking backwards in a straight line, or walk a "wide" serpentine allowing the handler to move to the left and right directing the dog.

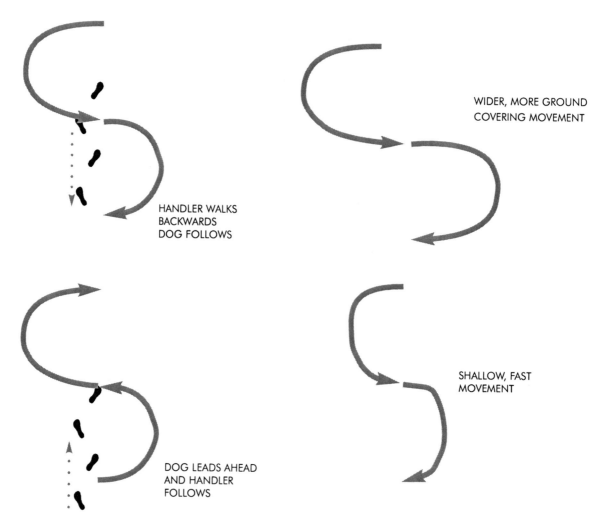

HANDLER WALKS
BACKWARDS
DOG FOLLOWS

WIDER, MORE GROUND
COVERING MOVEMENT

DOG LEADS AHEAD
AND HANDLER
FOLLOWS

SHALLOW, FAST
MOVEMENT

Identify in your own mind the movement the dog will do and in which direction. The dog can serpentine away from you as you follow the dog or towards you as you move backwards

The serpentine can also be "overturned" with a series of alternating circles, especial effective when the handler is walking backwards:

This move is easy to obtain once the dog has been taught to follow. It looks particularly graceful for the strong and easy gaiting dogs of any size. Collies can be disgusting at gaiting, it is not a "proper move" for a working dog, so for some it is hard to learn.

It is an excellent control exercise and useful to rest the dog between moves, easy on the spectator.

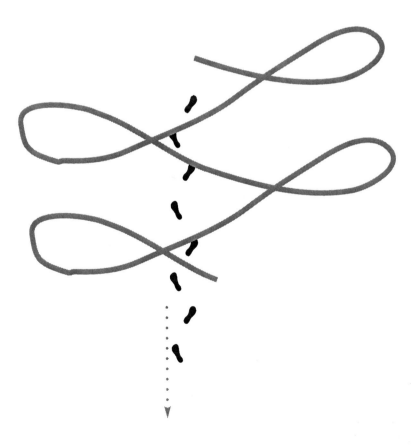

WEAVES

The dog will go under one leg come around to the front and go under the other leg. Variations on this depend whether the handler is walking forwards or backwards and the dog is turning to the front or the back.

Cue: **WEAVE OR THROUGH**
and bent leg signal to indicate which leg first.

As with the serpentine the size of the half circle can open up a whole range of very interesting moves. The dog can go through a "shallow" serpentine around legs walking fairly fast, or a large dog can walk a "wide" serpentine to allow the handler time to walk properly.

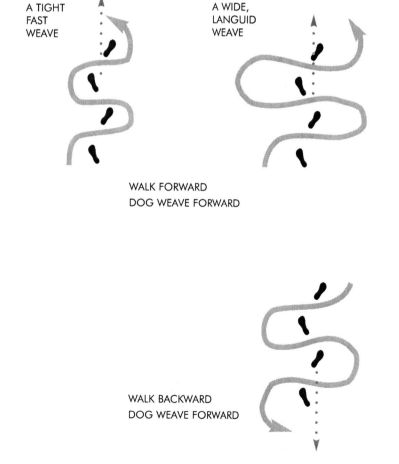

A TIGHT
FAST
WEAVE

A WIDE,
LANGUID
WEAVE

WALK FORWARD
DOG WEAVE FORWARD

WALK BACKWARD
DOG WEAVE FORWARD

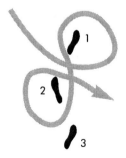

STEP FORWARD ON RIGHT LEG (1)
DOG GOES UNDER.
STEP BACK ONTO LEFT LEG (2), STEP
BACK ONTO RIGHT LEG (3),
DOG GOES UNDER LEFT LEG.

These are just for the dog walking forwards, we can also add the same range with the dog walking backwards.

For weaving the entry point and first cue will tell the dog which pattern to move, there are a lot of visual signals that make it quite easy for any dog to have a good range of weaving sets.

RECIPE 33 WEAVE TRAINING

The key when teaching the weave is to reward the dog for that first look under the leg, click and throw the food through the gap or you can use the target to lure the dog through.

DON'T, please DON"T bend over to lure the dog through, you'll look like you are try to scratch your backside. Equally don't use the hand signal as if you are pointing under you leg, it looks quite terrible!

Start with putting the "go under" leg on a chair or stool, and stay at the point until the dog goes under on first cue, click and lure the dog to front to reward. Gradually lower the leg to floor level, but retain your balance on the back leg. For larger dog if you can maintain the balance keep this leg bent and raised rather than open your legs wide to accommodate the dog. Think elegance!

Teach each direction separately, click on entry and fee around the front position. This rewards the dog for the hardest part (click) going under, and reinforces where to go when they have gone under with the food at the front.

CHANGING THE SHAPE

Weave patterns can also change shape with the way the handler moves, by placing the entry point and "leg under" at different points.

If the handler stands still, feet apart, the dog will complete a figure of eight turning to the front out of each turn or to the back.

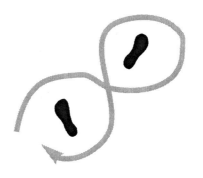

A similar move can be imitated by the handler standing with feet apart but one foot in front of the other, standing still, or changing weight from foot to foot. Only experimentation can give you good patterns but just remember to think of the variations of the dog's movement and what the dog needs to know.

RECIPE 34 BACKWARDS CIRCLES

Backing round in a circle, usually around you, one leg or an object. Free backing small circles can turn into twists and spins.

Cues: **RE-VERSE** anticlockwise
        UNDER clockwise

So far we have only taught the dog to back in a straight line, now we are going to bring in circles and curves. Use a shape or barrier box.

▶   Start with the dog standing across the front of you, their nose facing your right hand, tail in front of my left hand. (1)

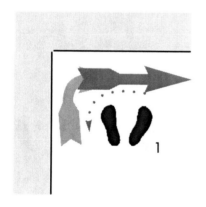

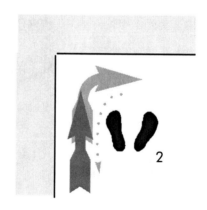

▶ Ask the dog to back into the heel position the dog will have to bend around the curve, pulling themselves into the location rear end first. (2)

Dogs will always find it easier to learn when the last part of the exercise or chain is taught first, then as you add on the next part the sequence gets stronger and stronger progressing onto familiar ground.

So firstly we teach the dog how to arrive into the hot spot around the bend. The next part will be to increase the amount of bend the dog goes around.

▶ Start with the dog on the right side position facing backwards, ask for the back movement and ensure the wall shapes the dog into curving around you. (3)

If you only have one corner to work in you will need to rotate yourself now to face the wall on your left, to ensure the dog completes the ... Ideally some ... aper".

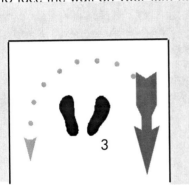

Now you can start with the dog standing behind you, with the rear end ready to come around on your right (4). I usually find the dogs will start to anticipate which is a good measure of their understanding.

This is one occasion where I separate the click from the reward, I click on the early understand of initiating the move, but only reward when they get back to the hot spot.

Soon you can start the dog off in the hot spot, make sure the wall is behind you to guide the weakest part of the circuit, click when you see them half way around, feed back in the hot spot.

Teach this from the other side in the same format and you will have a dog that can turn either circle to come backwards.

The dog is then ready to add the cue.

RECIPE 35 TEACHING THE BACK OFF, TURN AND BACK TOWARDS YOU

Be clear in your own mind which cue turns the dog which way and begin linking walking back away, with a turn and a back towards.

The dog understands the cue to reverse: "pull backwards to the right", and the dog will walk a circle anti-clockwise backwards around you.

▶ You can start this with the dog on your right side, facing behind you. Walk forward with the dog two or three steps, stand still and ask the dog to reverse, walk back two or three steps.

▶ If you can plan this to walk into your reverse barrier, it will be much easier for the dog to understand what they are going to do.

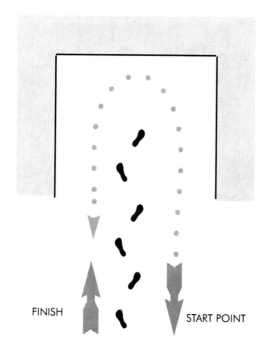

FINISH   START POINT

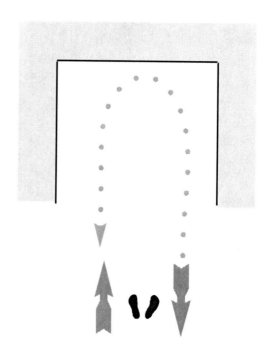

▶ The next step is to add strong verbal cues to each stage and start the dog off with one step, but let the dog continue by themselves.

When the dog arrives you can place yourself where it suits, ask the dog to go through you legs, or into the heel, side or front.

It looks quite cute if you let the dog go through your legs whilst you walk forwards, the dog then continues backwards and turn again to come towards you from behind.

RECIPE 36 BACKWARDS WEAVING

This is very similar to the ordinary weaving, in that it incorporates two sets of curves in different directions. The dog must be able to reverse and under full circles around you either way with equal strength.

In addition the dog must truly lead with their tail, and not do a flip around the front feet. This will cause them to swing wide and not get under the leg. The back must bend.

▶ Begin with the dog in the left heel position and ask for the Re-verse, except this time stand about a foot away from the wall with your back to the wall and your right heel against the wall

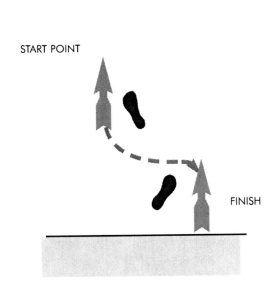

START POINT

FINISH

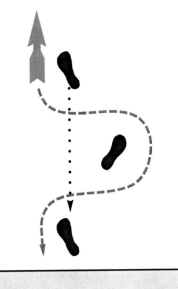

▶ Practise both sides to separately to equal fluency before putting together. To keep the flow the cue for changing the curve must be given as soon as the dog goes beneath your leg.

6 Poses

BOW

BEG

ROLL OVER

SLEEPY

Poses, or a held position, play an important part of any routine.

This is for most people a spectator activity, or certainly a partnership activity and an opening courtesy for your audience or partner is usually a bow or high five.

This can also serve as your opening pose. In competition one normally enters the ring and bows to the audience, the judges, your partner and then holds a position whilst waiting for the music to start. It can be the most excruciating part of the routine, "does my bum look big" is the least of your worries ...!!!!

All dogs need to learn to bow, or take a dip or even give a high five for success at the close of the routine.

During the routine the poses interrupt the flow, if this is carefully choreographed into the routine it can look very effective. There are often several occasions where you will stand still and the dog will be moving, this can be an opportunity for the reverse.

I have a Scottish dancing routine where Mabel adopts the bow and I dance around her, she can also place one foot over her eyes in this pose to add a bit of drama "ohmigod she's dancin' again". I don't quite have the nerve to adopt the canine version of the bow whilst she goes around me, since my bum DOES look big, very big!

So think about incorporating poses, they give the dog a break for a second, can add another dimension to the routine, but don't create a stoppage of both partners for more than about 10 seconds, the audience will be more captivated by the contrast to the movement.

Pose training will depend on the ability of the dog to be able to "be still", this is a foundation exercise, and once the dog has learned through the clicker communication the concept of "being still" then they will be able to transfer this to all situations. (Page 23).

BE OBSERVANT

Your dog's health is always more important that a "cool" new move. If you started yoga class next week you would not be expected to sit with your feet behind your head, that may take a year or two, or you may even never be able to do it since your hip structure would not allow for it.

The same with poses, the dog must develop through exercise, ligaments must be gently stretched and strength in the muscles built up slowly. Stretching exercises are useful for warming up, sustaining the stretch for a second of two longer each time will increase flexibility and suppleness. Strength can be built by adding a little more push, pull exertion.

But even with a careful building programme a dog that does not have the conformation to maintain the position carefully will never "get" the conformation, it is just the way the dog is built. A dog with unsound hips cannot be asked to maintain a high (upright) position without serious damage.

Logically you will think to yourself that if the dog can't do it or it cause pain then it simple won't do it. Wrong, collies are notorious for ignoring pain to get the job done, you will have to be their personal coach and guardian of their health.

Young dogs can appear to do the positions and sustain difficult moves, but any positions requiring strength should never be done with a collie under a year old and a larger dog under 18 months. They lack the smaller muscle structures and strengths you won't know the damage done until later in life.

Kiwi is far more supple and active at 9 than her mother was as the same age, dance training has certainly increased her body strength, fitness and mobility.

As with much exercise training is it the impact on landing that causes long term damage, especially if following a twisting movement.

Be careful, these dog are precious. Be observant, build slowly and read the dog's genuine ability.

BOWS AND BENDS

The dog can go into a play bow and be able to hold the position - backside high in the air, elbows on the floor. The longer backed breeds can sustain this easily, some of the shorter back dogs can only manage a dip.

Cue: **BEND, TAKE A BOW**

(the word bow can confuse "down" trained dogs)

The Gordon Setters are naturally "bow-ers" the give the play bow many times a day giving me the opportunity to capture it spontaneously. They can also comfortably maintain that position so I can add extra movements like the chin to the floor (sleepy) and the foot over the face (tired).

With Kiwi I tried very, very hard for the best part of a year to capture the bow, she just ended up hitting the deck soooo fast I was getting no where. So I went back to "assisted learning". I stood her on the grooming box - which is about my waist height, placed the left hand and clicker on the inside of her back leg nearest me, with the right hand took a piece of food via the nose to a point between her front legs.

A sustainable bow

RECIPE 37 TEACHING THE BOW

You are looking for the hinged movement around the elbows and shoulders, the dog's front feet will stay on the spot, so the head dips down between the front legs and the body generally moves backwards. To prevent the dog completing the movement into a down your other hand will stop the knee from bending. You don't have to hold the dog up by the stomach, just prevent the knee movement, keep it straight. This hand can also feel the pressure on that knee to move, a dog unused to this movement will initially want to drop the rear end as well, but regard it as a canine version of touching your toes, to start with it is not so easy, but once the spine and ligaments have been stretched little by little each day you will notice the knees less inclined to want to bend.

Kiwi learned this at the grand old age of nine and she was quite rigid to start with.

Quiz was shaped into a bow from an initial "dip" with the head, if she flopped into the down altogether I withheld the click, this faded away and I was left with a bow.

But.

Her version which she taught herself is a "stretch bow", the sort a dog does and walks forwards into after waking up. A great movement on it own, but it isn't a position she can sustain, so back to the "assisted learning" for that one!

You are likely to want this move with the hand signal as a cue or a bow from yourself, so learn how to bow ladies, take one step backwards and bend this knee, keep the other leg straight rocking the toes upwards, tuck in the backside, bend from the waist. Usually the arm on the same side as the straight front leg is tucked across the waist and the other arm is flourishing one's hat out to the side!

Keep it neat, mimic the dog's degree of bend and put the dog on your bow cue.

Remember that you will need to be able to cue the bow "in front" and by your side. In Front when bowing to each other, by your side when jointly bowing to the audience.

Quiz with the stretch bow

BEGS

The classic dog sitting upright with the front feet off the floor, the beg. You can add on paw positions for expression

Cue: **BEG**

with additional cues for paw positions

Some people are uncomfortable teaching a dog to beg, since they consider it looks degrading, but from the dog's view it is just another way to get a click and reward and the added bonus is the positive reaction from people.

We are used to seeing small dogs beg, but when a lumping great Gordon begs it always brings a laugh ... and doesn't he know it!

This is a great exercise for hip muscle development and strengthening the back muscles as the dog learns to balance.

You must NOT start this with any dog under 9 months old, their bones and muscles are not strong enough, Gordons at 18 months can just begin on this.

RECIPE 38 TEACHING THE BEG

This pose is based on a sound sit position. Always check the dog is upright on its hips and not slopped to one side.

To move from sit to beg there is a slight shift in balance. The dog will not appreciable "lift", but rather tuck their mid-back forwards as they take their shoulders back.

▶   Start with the lure, either hand or target stick and just teach the dog to maintain the sit, but stretch the nose up in the air to touch the lure, the front feet stay on the floor at this stage.

It is important to spend a bit of time securing this learning, since the dog will have to control their desire to either jump up or stand up to reach the lure.

> ▶ Gradually take the target further backwards, inch by inch. Let the dog just try to reach the target by taking one or both feet off the ground.

At this point the dog can start to wobble a bit, so again level out at this stage of learning to let the dog learn their balance, rather like riding a bike!

If the dogs are particularly wobbly, sit the dog and stand behind the dog as close as you can get, place your feet apart either side of the dog. The dog will now focus on you behind and above them and can rest against your legs for balance.

> ▶ Increase the amount of backwards movement until both feet are off the floor, some dogs may rest one paw against you for balance.

Quiz taught herself this as a paw based exercise and so begs with both feet raised, she used her paws on my lure hand to balance. I recommend you teach this with a target stick which tends to inhibit rising feet until you cue them after the beg is obtained.

CUTE BEGS

After you have taught the dog their paw work (in Smart Moves - Paws) you can add gestures which make this position more expressive. I think we are rather coloured by Disney's version of an embarrassed dog, we train them to put their feet over their face. If a dog is embarrassed it simply looks away, if its feet are on its face it is to wipe off the food for cleaning!

This sort of paw work can be carried out in sit or down, but only both feet can be employed in the beg or upside down pose.

Some ideas:

WAVE - one paw can easily be held up in this position, make sure the dog can free stand and hold up a paw and then incorporate into the beg.

WASH - where both feet waggle, you can get this by clicking on paw movements.

TIRED - eye wiping, where the dog places one or both feet over the eyes. And they seem to be quite happy to block out all vision!

PRAYING - where the dog dips their head into their chest with both feet over their face, or on their head, some dogs look more effective if their feet are balanced against something, it allows a deeper head dip.

MEER CAT - where the front legs just dangle. Rather embarrassingly most dogs (boys) legs dangle in region of their willy, so be particularly careful where you demonstrate this move!

HI-FIVE BEG, this is an excellent held pose for dogs who find the solo beg a difficulty. Once the dog is beginning to rise ask for a paw to a hi-five hand, or both hands, and let the dog balance with this contact.

HI FIVE FROM BEHIND - this is suitable for dogs whose beg position brings them up to waist height. Stand behind the dog ask for the beg and put one hand out in front of the dog for the dog to rest a paw on. Also darned cute if the dog can maintain this contact whilst you walk around.

Holding a prop - extra "cutie" if the dog can bring you and item and beg with it, "please sir, may I have some more?"

aaaahhhh ....

DEAD DOGS

The dog will lie immobile on the floor on their side, or upside down. Extra paw moves can be added, such as tired, or a wave

Cue: **FALL OVER, FLAT** - to one side
ROLL- for the upside down

I suppose I am rather superstitious and I don't like to use the word "die" or "dead" for this exercise, just me being silly!

Both of these positions are part of the whole "rollover" movement and you can capture the position by inhibiting the rolling over action.

If the dog is fluent on the roll over, then use the click to mark the upside down position.

If the dog is rewarded after they have completed the roll then the dog will simply get faster and faster as soon as they hear the click, to make sure that as you click you hand is immediately there to give the dog the food in the position. This will then have the effect of freezing them or slowing them down when they hear the click.

Watch the dogs don't choke, they seem to manage to eat upside down - if they are relaxed!

I also help this "freeze" position by asking for both paws once they have rolled to this point, place your hand above their face and by targeting the paws to your hand you have effectively stopped the roll. Gordons often sleep in this position with a front leg straight up in the air.

The up stretching of the legs add a bit more drama to the idea of a stone dead dog!

RECIPE 39 ROLLOVER BY LURE & SHAPING

You can just as easily teach these poses as the beginning of a complete rollover, taking the dog gently through each step, rather than stressing them with the complete movement.

▶ from the down position, click and reward the dog for shifting their hips to one side.

Which ever way the hips have shifted is the way they will roll onto their back

▶ lure their head towards their elbow and ribs completing a "C" shape with the dog body, click and the dogs begins to rest on its shoulder.
or

▶ shape by letting the dog sink to the side they will roll onto, the dog will shift onto its shoulder.

A lie flat position is primarily achieved with the hips going "flat" and then the shoulders.

Always make sure the dog gets to this position via the down position and does not throw itself onto a shoulder from standing.

- ▶ Some dogs can be easily lured into the "roll" upside down with promise of belly rubs, so just a hint of a fuss on the appropriate part and you are often presented with the move. Clicking and reward by belly rubs.

- ▶ If the dog is not tempted, continue the lure to elbow movement by bring the dogs head over its ribs. A dog must slightly curl its body into a "C" shape to roll onto its back, unless it is too fat!

I separate the "rollover" into these movements, which give me additional poses without additional cues.

"**ROLL**" = upside down   "**OVER**" = stand up again

SLEEPY AND TIRED

Sleepy in the down position with the dog's chin on the floor. Tired is the same move with the dog's feet over their eyes as well.

Cue: **SLEEPY?   TIRED?**

RECIPE 40 SLEEPY

With the dog in the down position you will click every dip of the head. Make sure you deliver the titbit so that the dog can maintain the down position.

This start from just minute dips of their head and requires you to WAIT for it to happen, I find it an excellent shaping exercise since you can focus the dog on a single movement of one part of their body, so many moves we teach are complex and the dog is often confused by what they just did with what to appreciate the principles of marking and shaping.

You can let the dog rest their head on a paw, but this will inhibit the "tired" pose.

Each time as the dog builds confidence, withhold the click very, very slightly longer, not so much that the dog tries something else, but enough to stretch the length of the pose.

You will help the dog with this exercise if you are sitting in a chair or on the floor with the dog, they can maintain eye contact easier.

Awake is the opposite move to "sleepy", ie once you have asked the dog to put their head down, they begin to think that every down should be accompanied by a "sleepy". Once the sleepy is on cue, then when the dog lifts it head up, but maintains the down, that becomes the "a-wake".

RECIPE 41 TIRED

I like to teach this exercise in the sleepy or down position, the rest of the dog's body is "sorted" and they only have to learn to move one leg, no shifting balance or dipping their head.

Starting from a good "sleepy", which the dog can maintain:

▶ You can stimulate the dog to put a paw over their face by blowing gently on their eyebrow. BUT … be aware that some dogs will jump up at your face at the same time, thinking this is a good game, black eye territory.

▶ The old Disney dogs would learn this with a piece of tape, like sellotape over the bridge of their face. I tried it with Quiz and I think she thought bugs were crawling up her face. But it may be the break through for one dog.

▶ You can also place some dinner on the dog's face, most will use their paws like a cat to clean up and it is self rewarding!

▶ Shaping from the sleepy is straightforward, just withhold the click and wait for a foot to move, they seem to place it naturally over their nose or eyes, or you can hint with the paw cue.

7 Tricky Stuff

PAW WORK

HI WORK

JUMPS

CREEP

PAWS

The foundation move teaches the dogto tap each front paw against the palm of the handand then wave the paw on cue.

Cue: **TICK** = left foot
      TOCK = right foot
      BOTH = both feet

Paw training is excellent for teaching the dog awareness of its feet, balance and it is the basis of them understanding their left from right.

Many of the moves we do can be explained to the dog a little better if we could clearly give a "to your left" cue in conjunction with the movement:

"CIRCLE - to you right"

"ROLLOVER - to your left

"HEEL - with me on your right"

"SIDE STEP -   to your left etc.

We are just waiting for a person and dog full of energy to test this out! Certainly Quiz rollovers with a hand signal, and she rolls to the direction "of that hand", ie the leg she drops onto is the same side as the hand, the same side as for a paw wave.

Paw movements will be cued individually, the left and the right separate and the both paws as a third cue. Remember that when the dog is facing you the paw cues are reversed for when the dog is by your side.

We can also put paw cues onto feet, target sticks and other objects.

RECIPE 42 PAW TAP

I think this is most effectively taught by part lure and part natural reaction, although there are some dogs who may be better shaped.

▶   sit on the floor with the dog in the sit in front of you

▶   take a piece of food in the palm of your hand and close the fist, only loosely, allow the scent of the food to escape

- ▶ place the fist, WITH THE BACK OF YOUR HAND to the floor, make sure the hand is next to the paw on the same side, not crossing over.

- ▶ let the dog sniff the fist, let the tongue wiggle through the fingers and get a taste. The frustration of not being able to get the food will stimulate the dog to try with a foot.

- ▶ if you are quick off the mark click on the gentlest of taps, at the same time the hand springs open for the food reward.

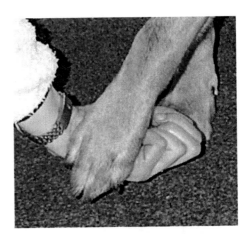

Be warned that if you let the dog get too enthusiastic about digging the food out of the hand, they will always tend to use their paws with all claws extended - this can get extremely painful on the shins, the feet, the hands, the arms etc.

Use the click slightly in advance of the contact to inhibit the power. The hand signal will become a cue for the paw, not a smack.

- ▶ Only use the food to stimulate the paw for about 3 efforts, then mimic the collection of the food and go through exactly the same gestures but food free. Click on contact, collect the titbit with the fist hand - don't swap cue hand and delivery hand it is too confusing!

- ▶ As soon as the dog is tapping an empty fist, begin to very slowly open the hand, you will gradually change the cue for "paw" to palm not fist.

- ▶ Once the dog is fluent on one side then swop hands and work on the other.

This is one of the exercises that is tricky with a clicker since swapping hands and paws is an essential part of the learning and the dog can watch you swop the clicker prior to your signal. If you have another pair of hands available utilise them to teach the next part.

- ▶ Now teach the dog to alternate paws, this will mean they have to keep changing their balance. An essential skill for progress.

RECIPE 43 PAW WAVE

Up to this point the dogs have "hit the spot" and received food. Make an effort to change this to a wave as soon as possible otherwise the dog will become conditioned that they HAVE to make contact, not just "use the paw".

Find a way to prevent the dog reaching your hand, these are some of the choices:

> ▶ Sit the dog on a box, or table and give plenty of reward for being there - feed on the box and secure in their mind that this is the only place they will get reward. The dog needs to stop itself coming off the box.

> ▶ Turn your hand the other way up for a high five and stay within reach so that the dog successfully touches. Click and reward.

> ▶ As the dog goes to swipe your hand take it away. Click for the lack of contact and reward.

> ▶ Take a step backwards, give the signal, let the dog reach but click before they fall off the box. Always return to the box to reward.

> ▶ Spend a little time here having a look at the shape of the paw. I like a good stretched paw with a big gesture for contact, a high held paw for the wave and a tucked under paw for a "poorly paw". They all have different cues.

The contact paw will continue to be palm of hand.

The high wave paw will be cued by a high five hand - ie the fingers pointing upwards with the palm facing the dog, given about shoulder height.

The tucked under paw is cued by the bent wrist and the back of the hand showing to the dog ... I think this may also be described as "limp wristed" I give this signal at about waist height.

> ▶ Modify the hand signal and shape all three movements with each hand. They are essential as

foundation movements for some really cool moves later on.

By this time you should also be standing facing the dog, training them on a box can encourage them to sit but this makes paw changes easier for the dog to concentrate on.

Practice each hand/paw alternately, if you have no second pair of hands for clicking as you swop use a small bug clicker under your foot. Food is collected on success.

You can change to foot cues to be able to match the dog's kick with your own stride.

- ▶ Take off your shoes and put them on your hands, click and reward for contacting the shoe. Start with the dog on the box to inhibit the smack.

- ▶ Put your shoes back on, take the box away so the dog is on the floor - cue the dog with the foot in the shoe.

This is also a great time to unlock the dog out of sitting for paw work. So when you give the foot cue make sure the dog steps towards you to make contact, this will ensure that the sitting does not continue.

Don't forget to transfer the learning to the side or heel location. Choose either of both of these options, they each have their advantages:

- ▶ Use the "tick and tock" cues to signal to the feet.

- ▶ Use the foot signal to cue the feet.

It will depend whether you want the dog to look at you or not. If I cue Mabel with my feet then she needs to look at them, so I lightly touch my inside hand on her back to cue her to look at the shoes.

Collies don't seem to need to look a shoes - they are smart enough to read the changing balance you give when you march on the spot!

BUILDING YOUR REPERTOIRE

How many of these moves you choose to teach is up to you. Some dogs are very dexterous with their paws and enjoy a range of moves, whereas others will be limited.

RECIPE 44 FLYING HI-FIVES

A cross between a hi-five for "both" paws and a running jump. Give the two hands hi-five signal and allow plenty of room for the dog to take a jump upwards.

To add drama to this move it is essential to put it on a verbal cue.

Visually the timing of your hand signal, then the dog jumping would be out of sync. Plan to give the verbal cue and then join the dog as is rises for the Flying Hi Five so that you both appear to raise together. Looks very dramatic.

RECIPE 45 KICK WALK

This can be either by your side or the dog coming towards you,
I also add the crossed leg when the dog comes towards me,
they still match your foot to paw and cross their leg over as well.

Kick behind walk where the dog walks along behind you
tapping each foot or your hand held behind you.

These movements looks great when they are confidence and so
well practised that they happen without delay or effort.

RECIPE 46 HI WALK

Hi Walk, the high move, is the dog up on its back legs. This is
taught very easily with a target stick.

The dog find their balance easier to maintain by moving very
slightly backwards. To exercise the hips and back leg muscles, I
like to stretch the dog from a good sitting position, up into a
beg and then straight up into the Hi Walk. Several weeks of 2 or
3 of these a day and the dog will be able to sustain this
position, walk and turn.

Once a comfortable balance is obtained you can merge many
other poses and movements into this:

> Wave - for either or both feet

> Tired - to sink the head into the feet

> Walk back - moving back away from you or reversing

> Heel - dog in the heel but up by your shoulder

Hopping is the easier way for some dogs to move forwards.

But, perlease, don't ask your dog to stand Hi behind you and
follow you. From a spectator point of view the description has to
encompass the words: "dignity" and "lack of".

ROLLOVERS

The dog will drop to roll over from the down position, in either direction and come out of the move to standing again.

Cue: **ROLLOVER**
with hand cue for which direction

From the health aspect this needs to be taught in both directions, a great exercise for strengthening the stomach and back muscles - and good for grooming and undercarriage inspections

Before you can teach this you must observe that the dog is comfortable and able to roll over of their own volition. Some dogs hardly ever roll, perhaps because it is physically uncomfortable or perhaps because they are anxious at being in such a vulnerable position. Sometimes a dog will roll at home, on carpet, but not in a strange place or poor surface. It is a security linked movement - and a full stomach moment as well!

I will use the hand signal as if "give me the paw on that side", ie the same side as the hand signal, to indicate to the dog which shoulder to drop onto, which way to roll.

If the dog is "in front" in the down, I give the left hand palm indicating her right paw, she will roll to my left. I keep the hand signal up and sweep it out to the side to indicate this is a roll and go movement, not the roll and stop halfway movement.

RECIPE 47 ROLLOVER

You can either shape or lure for this, shaping secures the understanding in the dog's mind more than luring.

SHAPING

- ▶ Begin with the down and reward the dog for the hip roll. This moves their spine closed to the floor on one side, this is the direction the roll will take.

- ▶ The next move is the dog dropping onto one shoulder. Secure the hip roll and withhold until the dog sinks slightly more, they can also achieve this by raising the "top" back leg or turning their heads back slightly as if they were going to do a spin or twirl.

▶ Once they have reached half way point, move yourself behind the dog so that when you click they naturally complete the roll over to return to you.

LURING

▶ Start at the same point as for shaping and place yourself to the side of the dog. Lure the hip roll by moving their head backwards to their elbow, encouraging a nice "C" shape, click and the hip roll and feed without the dog getting up.

▶ Don't aim to get the full roll over in one session, but just build the dog mobility through increasing this "C" shape and the same time begin to roll the "C" onto its back.

▶ Once you reach this stage it is better that you position yourself to the side the dog will roll to, to lure the dog right over and out of the upside down position.

The only danger with the movement is the dog's haste to begin the roll means they throw themselves onto one shoulder. Not good. Always encourage them to a clean drop before they roll.

It will help if you teach roll in both directions then they will not be so likely to drop continuously on one side.

The cue for the dog to roll to their right, your left, will be the left hand cue with the verbal, and the opposite for the other direction. This is useful when the dog is "in front" and the choice is open either way.

If the dog is at your side or heel position, then your rollover cue in that context can either mean roll away or roll towards me - if they roll towards then you will have to shift, over the top or step away.

JUMPS

The choice is very varied :

> the classic curved jump over a prop or leg

> the spring up in the air

> the bounce

Cue: **OVER**   **UP** **POP**

Jumping is great way to express key points in the music, adding that extra emphasis, but it is also probably the way you are most likely to injure you dog.

Safety notes to remind yourself:

▶ Do not jump young dogs, their bones are still soft and landing can permanently injure. Dogs don't think about landing!

▶ Always jump on a kind surface, where the take off is without slipping and the landing also slip free and with some impact absorption. Carpet over a good rubber underlay is suitable - but mind the carpet burns!

▶ Teach the dog how control itself in the jump. Just because is "gets over" the pole does not mean it is jumping to the best of its ability or healthily.

▶ Don't ask for twisting in the jumps at all.

RECIPE 48 JUMPS

As always you need to focus firstly on getting the behaviour. In this case the behaviour is not necessarily a successful jump. Teach the dog to jump a small pole, very easy height, no higher that the dog's elbow.

By conditioning the dog at this stage that a jump is a graceful vertically curved motion, not plop over, flip, side hop, lamb spring or any thing else, then the dog will jump soundly on more difficult challenges.

Make sure the dog is jumping with purpose in a straight line forwards, do not stand to the side of the jump with a clicker as the dog will turn to you as it hears the click.

JUMPING YOU

Set up the jump so that you can place yourself adjacent, the dog is already conditioned to jumping the pole, so just place to pole over the relevant body part you want the dog to jump:

▶ Sit by the jump and place your leg under the jump horizontally. You may need to balance like a Russian Cossack, but just think of the exercise!

▶ Place your arm under the pole, or even lie under the pole if you want the dog to jump you, this is best achieved with that extra pairs of hands your have near by.

Do not underestimate the benefit of some agility training to get the dog really fit and confident in jumping, it can make all the difference.

You can also use your arms as a ring for the dog to jump through, take a hoop for the dog or skipping rope.

At all times keep the dog really straight, if you are asking the dog to jump arms or legs, remember centrifugal force will pull the dog away from you, so make sure your arm or leg is against a wall to keep the dog close to you.

SPRINGS AND POPS

Quite a lot of dogs spring naturally and as in jumping the responsibility is on you to make sure the dog is doing it safely.

I know I keep beating the drum about safety, you only have to see one dog fatally cripple itself with a bad twisting jump to take the extra time to warn everyone about TAKING CARE

Most Genabacabs (my affix) come with a built in spring but their action is a vertical spring which can, and has, damaged front feet. They like to punch the ground for attention. So I always control this by keeping the height modest and only ask for it on good surfaces and when needed.

I teach the spring jump the non-built bouncers with a hi-five cue. It looks more dramatic with the dog's front feet extended.

BOUNCING

Kiwi's daughter Quiz has her own version of the Genabacab spring - but she only does to gain speed going backwards, I think it gives her more oomph.

A bounce is the front feet coming off the ground together and working as one unit. You can put it on cue with the target stick.

Capturing the right rhythm for this is very important.

LAMB BOUNCE

Yep, watch lambs the next time out, this is a spring up in the air off all four feet and landing on all four feet, the dog's back stays horizontal to the floor, although some seem to make a curved shape out of it.

Once the dog has a sound plain jump take the pole and hold it by one end in front of you. Stand the dog by the side of the pole and ask it to pop over sideways. We are talking very low poles here, perhaps 6 - 12 inches off the ground, you are only try to capture a particular action, not break the record for side jumping dogs.

Once the dog has the action on cue and on a hand signal, take the pole away and stand up, give the cue and the dog will jump. Initially there may be some sideways movement, but that is what your clicker is for - to explain to the dog that it doesn't matter any more.

PUSH-OFF

You've got to be brave or mad for this one!

For the daring people you are going to teach your dog to run at you, hit you and bounce off - probably above waist height to make it effective!

The human flyball box! It is pretty easy to achieve on the same principles, you will reward your dog for jumping up to start with, and then increase the distance. But a collie travelling at a modest speed can hit with quite a clout, so you will need to brace yourself.

JUMP IN MY ARMS

Aaaaahhhh ... always good for the spectators, the dog will need confidence that you won't "miss" when you go for the catch!

CREEP

The dog travels along the ground maintaining the down position, and believe it or not they can do it backwards as well as forwards!

Cue: **CREEP OR CRAWL**

This is not the exercise for every dog, they will have to be quite fit, agile, flexible and young!

You will teach the dog to progress along the ground forwards which means the front legs will do a sort of shuffle/pulling action and the back legs a mixture of push and hopping.

The dogs will sort out their own bodies to achieve this.

RECIPE 49 TEACHING CREEP

I think this is best taught by luring, either hand food or target, you will need to make sure the dog maintains a upright "lion" down and not tries to fall to one side or the other, otherwise we could call it a grovel!

▶ Start the dog in the down, place the lure at ground level and forwards, click the dog for the forward movement.

▶ Transfer the lure from hand to target stick as soon as possible then you can stand up.

This can add an extra dimension to the routine, as jumps can fill another level, so can close ground work, but make sure when you teach it that you do not have to bend over the dog to cue it. You can also ask the dog to creep weave.

There may be a dramatic effect where the dog creeps along in the side or heel position and you mimic the dog, but generally aim to have this on voice cue, lots of bending over the dog does not present a polished performance.

RECIPE 50 BACKWARD CREEP

I came across the by accident, some wonderful movements can arrive out of total confusion and misinterpretation!

I had taught all the Gordons to Back-off, an essential exercise for brain management when they purposefully gang up on me for a mugging, this was taught before the litter dispersed and therefore a strong conditioned movement = "take a few steps away from me".

I was training Arnold in the down for his "repertoire" and wanted him to stand up - so as with all the previous learners I gave the "back-up" cue, which usually stands the dog with a back pulling motion.

Except ...... he start shuffling backwards in the down. It looks rather like he is trying to limbo since he rocks from side to side, and it is almost impossible on carpet, but worth playing around with!

He pumps his front feet vigorously as if in a temper tantrum ... unfortunately lots of vocals accompany it as well!

CONTACTS:

In the UK:

The sport is recognised as Heelwork to Music, details can be obtained from the Kennel Club, I Clarges Street, Piccadilly. London W1Y 8AB

www.paws-n-music.com
for competitions, progress awards and training days

www.maryray.co.uk
for a superb range of teaching and demonstration videos

In the USA:

The sport is usually called Freestyle:

www.musicaldogsport.org

www.canine-freestyle.org

www.worldcaninefreestyle.org

Groups are training worldwide in New Zealand, Australia, Germany, Italy, Switzerland, Belgium, Holland, Scandinavia, Canada.

Where ever clicker trainers meet they soon begin to play the music.

Clicker Clips
with Kay Laurence

with help from Arnold, Kent, Mabel, Ivy, Quiz and Kiwi and Tip. "Team Genabacab"

One hour of video clips ranging from teaching new behaviours to the practice sessions for established behaviours. Video in VHS PAL or VHS NTSC.

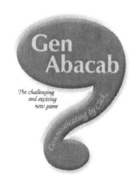

Recipe books for specialised interests in:

Clicker Competition Obedience teaching precise and accurate obedience exercises.

Clicker Agility* for fun and fitness.

Clicker Ringcraft* for show dogs.

Book of Challenges for Foundation and Novice Level trainers

for details of all publications and training gear:

UK: Learning About Dogs Ltd,
       PO Box 13, Chipping Campden
       Glos GL55 6WX

USA: Karen Pryor ClickerTraining
       49 River Street, Waltham, MA 02453
       www.clickertraining.com
       U.S. Toll Free 800-472-5424
       781-398-075

www.clickertraining.com

FROM

Learning About Dogs

TEACHING DOGS Magazine

Training for all types of companion, working and sports dogs

POSITIVE LEARNING FOR POSITIVE RESULTS

CAP Certification at 4 levels

648599

Made in the USA